Presenting MAGIC CAP™

A Guide to General Magic's Revolutionary Communicator Software

Barbara Knaster

Addison-Wesley Publishing Company
Reading, Massachusetts • Menlo Park, California
New York • Don Mills, Ontario • Wokingham, England
Amsterdam • Bonn • Sydney • Singapore • Tokyo
Madrid • San Juan • Paris • Seoul • Milan
Mexico City • Taipei

Many of the designations used by manufacturers and sellers to distinguish their products are claimed as trademarks. Where those designations appear in this book, and Addison-Wesley was aware of a trademark claim, the designations have been printed in initial capital letters or all capital letters.

The author and publishers have taken care in preparation of this book, but make no expressed or implied warranty of any kind and assume no responsibility for errors or omissions. No liability is assumed for incidental or consequential damages in connection with or arising out of the use of the information or programs contained herein.

Library of Congress Cataloging-in-Publication Data

Knaster, Barbara.
   Presenting Magic Cap : a guide to General Magic's revolutionary communicator software / Barbara Knaster.
      p. cm.
   Includes index.
   ISBN 0-201-40740-X
   1. Communications software.   2. Magic cap.   I. Title.
TK5105.9.K58   1994
650.1'0285'5369—dc20   93-46018
                                                              CIP

Sponsoring Editor: Martha Steffen
Project Manager: Joanne Clapp Fullagar
Production Coordinators: Vicki Hochstedler • Gail McDonald
   Jordan
Cover design: Grand Design/Boston
Set in 11 point Serifa Light by Total Concept Associates

1 2 3 4 5 6 7 8 9-ARM-9897969594
First printing, February 1994

Addison-Wesley books are available for bulk purchases by corporations, institutions, and other organizations. For more information please contact the Corporate, Government and Special Sales Department at (800) 238-9682.

Contents

For my boys,
Scott and Jess

Preface

 **About Magic Cap**

Why Me?

I don't love technology. I don't hate it either, but I don't welcome it into my life unless I can figure out how it will make me happier or more efficient. I think of this as being very practical, but since I live in Silicon Valley, some people consider me almost primitive for having this attitude.

When I first heard about General Magic's dream of creating a personal communicator, I was impressed by the team of programming and user interface legends who had been assembled to build this portable box that kept you in touch all the time. At the same time, I wondered why most people would want one of these things. These communicators were going to let you send messages to anyone from anywhere, and they were going to be as easy to use as a telephone. Well, I already had a telephone, and I sometimes found it more intrusive than indispensable.

A personal communicator would also be an electronic datebook and notepad. There were plenty of electronic organizers already; would this one be just another expensive toy? I seemed to have no trouble at all being skeptical, wondering whether this idea of "reinventing telephony" would have much of an impact in the real world outside Silicon Valley, even with the impressive track record of the wizards at General Magic.

Of course, the list of companies that helped get General Magic rolling (Sony, Motorola, and Apple) and the others who joined along the way (AT&T, Philips, and Matsushita) added a lot to this tiny start-up company's credibility. Eventually, I became a guinea pig in official tests of the software in General Magic's lab and unofficial tests at home, courtesy of my husband, who joined the team as employee number 14. As the communicator shaped up, I started to see for the first time how it might fit into my life.

I also became intrigued by the powerful culture of this unique company: dedicated workaholics collaborated with engineers who had families, sharing an almost fanatical need to make magic. Watching this culture work to make practical tools helped convert my skepticism into enthusiasm. General Magic's dreams developed into two software platforms: Magic Cap and Telescript.

Origins of General Magic

The original idea for personal communicators sprouted in Apple's Advanced Technology Group. A research group led by Marc Porat observed three central trends that showed how people spent their work and personal time. First was the need to communicate easily and conveniently—with co-workers in the same office, with a spouse running errands, with clients in other parts of the world. Second, people increasingly require information on demand—stock quotes, movie schedules, how the home team fared. The third trend was remembering all this information—who to meet, where to be, when to be there. Porat also proposed the theory that people don't always clearly separate the personal and business parts of their day, which is the root of what he calls *whole person thinking*.

Creating a product for this model was the challenge. The code name Paradigm was chosen for the project (you can't do anything in Silicon Valley without a code name). When Apple realized that it couldn't devote enough resources to the Paradigm project, General Magic was created in 1990. The founders of the company were Marc Porat, the visionary who nurtured the ideas and put together the astonishing alliance of consumer electronics manufacturers and communications giants; Bill Atkinson, the legendary programmer and user interface designer who created HyperCard and the original graphics software in the Macintosh; and Andy Hertzfeld, the software wizard who programmed much of the original Macintosh. In subsequent years, many talented programmers and designers who worked on other successful products joined General Magic to form a world-class engineering group.

It's the Communication

The whole idea of Magic Cap is communication. A personal organizer is cool, but it's been done. An electronic datebook and address book combination is really useful, but it's not necessarily more special than its paper counterpart. Electronic mail and information services aren't just trendy, last-minute additions to Magic Cap; from the beginning of the project, everything in Magic Cap was designed around the idea of enabling people to communicate powerfully and easily.

When you turn on a Magic Cap communicator, you see a picture of a desk, laid out to simulate the way people work (see Figure P-1). There's a telephone, a datebook, a file for names and addresses, a notebook for writing and drawing. But right in the middle of the desk is a postcard and pencil, a subtle reminder of what Magic Cap is all about. The in box and out box are also located in the center of the communicator's screen, their prominent positions drawing your eyes and attention.

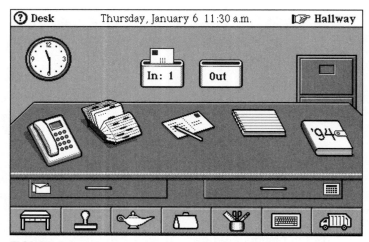

FIGURE P-1. The Magic Cap desk

Placing the postcard and other kinds of stationery in the desk drawer, Magic Cap encourages you to use electronic mail for every purpose: business letters to prospective clients, personal notes to your mom, invitations to meetings, birthday greetings to a friend in another state, and electronic orders for goods and services. You can use Magic Cap's electronic communication for many of the things you're used to doing with your telephone or postal service.

Every Magic Cap device is truly a communicator and not a message pad, an organizer, or a personal digital assistant. Every Magic Cap communicator comes ready to connect to a telephone line: there's a modem built in. Some also include two-way radios for wireless communication, but at the least, every Magic Cap communicator is only a standard telephone jack away from connecting you to the world of electronic networks.

Your communicator does a great job of replacing your address book, but it has another purpose for the names and addresses it knows: It can help you send messages to the people and companies it lists. Magic Cap also simulates your appointment book, and you can use it to contact the participants in your meetings to invite them to attend. Because Magic Cap's smart communication features connect you to the world outside, you can actually tell a news service what kinds of stories you're interested in, and those stories will be culled automatically and delivered for you to read at your convenience. Information providers may someday offer news, up-to-the-minute sports scores, movie and television schedules, road directions for many major cities, and lots of other services that somebody somewhere is dreaming up right now. It's like a home shopping network in the palm of your hand.

It's for Everybody

The engineers and interface designers at General Magic worked hard to make Magic Cap very easy to use. They wanted to make a consumer electronics product, not a computer, and so it had to be far easier to use than the simplest personal computer. There are lots of things that personal computers do very well, including keeping track of big chunks of data, publishing documents, and crunching numbers. Even though Magic Cap can handle some of those things, it was born to communicate.

Sending messages using AT&T's new PersonaLink service or conventional electronic mail and fax is intuitively simple with a communicator. Receiving mail is also easy—a matter of simply connecting and collecting. Because Magic Cap communicators are electronics products designed for general consumer use, they may not be as powerful as many personal computers, but they are certainly more friendly.

Magic Cap's designers conducted scores of user tests to refine the way it works. Features that were confusing to novice users were tweaked or simplified. For example, at one time users could move objects around on the desk just by sliding them. This was disconcerting to people who didn't have computer experience—they just wanted to open the datebook, but it kept scooting away instead. The designers made a trade-off: Users had to enter an explicit mode to be able to slide the permanent features on their desks, so savvy users could redecorate, but beginners wouldn't be startled by something happening unexpectedly.

Computer veterans and other knowledgeable users had suggestions for ways to increase power, and many of those suggestions were added to Magic Cap, but never at the expense of friendliness. Magic Cap's inventors included many features that make it easier for power users, but those features are designed to stay out of the way of beginners.

Magic Cap's navigation system is an example of the designers' focus on simplicity. It lets users work with a desk, rooms in a hallway, and a downtown street. Novice users inevitably love Magic Cap's navigation, and pundits often criticize its appearance as too simplistic and playful. Many experts also criticized the friendly, playful Macintosh interface when it appeared in 1984. Now, of course, most personal computer users work with windows, icons, menus, and other elements that were disparaged on the first Macintosh. We'll have to wait and see what the eventual response is to Magic Cap's interface.

Designers of products that are supposed to be easy to use often talk about whether "your parents" could use it. Magic Cap may not be as easy as a telephone, but it's designed so that most parents could quickly figure out how to use it to send a message to their children asking why they never write anymore.

Telescript Inside

Magic Cap integrates many tools that people use to communicate for work and play. At the core of this platform is Telescript, a communication-oriented programming language also developed by General Magic. There are several elements in the communication heart of Telescript. Foremost is its smart-messaging capability. As the foundation for sending and receiving electronic mail, Telescript actually turns each message into an agent, or independent program, that can carry personalized information with it.

Because each message is really a Telescript program, these "smart messages" can perform functions besides just expressing your words. If you use your communicator's datebook to schedule a meeting with your colleague Tony, you can also automatically create an invitation for him to attend the meeting, send it to him, and then have the message complete a series of reactions based upon his response; he can use it to create and deliver his acceptance or regrets, and even schedule the meeting in his datebook.

Telescript messages travel in "smart envelopes," which are Telescript programs that include a way to tell the message how to deliver itself. An electronic mail network based on Telescript can let you tell the message to wait in Tony's mailbox until 5 P.M., and if he doesn't pick it up by then, to fax it to him at home. The mailboxes that the message passes through are also Telescript programs, meaning that they're also smart and can carry personal preferences.

Using a Telescript-based network, you can stamp your message to Tony as urgent. Meanwhile, because his mailbox is also a Telescript program, he has instructed it to let him know immediately when he receives an urgent message. A conventional electronic mail system may also have some of these "smart" features, but if they weren't built into the original engineering, it would be impossible for users to add them later. If a Telescript system needs to add features, users of the mail system can add and revise them.

As more Telescript-based systems are created, they'll help extend the power of Magic Cap. A smart network would provide a handy way to interact with a store that has an electronic location downtown. If you wanted to send flowers to your Aunt Dorothy, you could visit the flower store downtown, then send a message to the florist that you wanted a bouquet of flowers for $35 to be delivered today in Kansas. Your order could automatically attach your name for billing and your aunt's name and address for delivery information. The flower shop's mailbox could have special rules set up for receiving such orders that would expedite having the flowers delivered in time for her birthday. So far, Magic Cap's engineers haven't figured out how to have the flowers themselves come through a communicator, but just wait.

Families of Products

There are several different models of Magic Cap communicators from different manufacturers, and each one provides ways to communicate. Some Magic Cap communicators need to be plugged into a phone line; others take advantage of wireless transmission via radio waves. There may be additional options like telephone handsets that plug into your communicator or cellular phones that can be added. Every one of these, though, has one thing in common: Magic Cap. Communication à la Magic Cap is the foundation; your distinctive model of communicator provides the access.

Design Goals

General Magic engineers worked together with their alliance partners in designing various models of communicators that had to meet important goals. Communicators have to be small enough to be carried around all the time and easy enough for people to figure them out without hours of study. Magic Cap's designers compensated for small screen size by making items look simple and easily touchable. Performing various tasks in Magic Cap is intuitive and easy: touch the screen to activate items on a desk, go into a hallway of rooms filled with other features, or go to a downtown street with buildings representing remote services.

The immaturity of touch-screen technology provides another design challenge. Screens of current models are often difficult to see, another reason that the desk items are spaced far apart and well defined. Because it's hard to touch an exact point, Magic Cap allows for an imprecise touch to act precisely.

Magic Cap uses an on-screen keyboard as its main source of input; its interface doesn't require handwriting recognition. Because an on-screen keyboard is unwieldy, Magic Cap includes a large set of features to speed up typing. These features include trying to automatically complete words in well-known categories (names, cities, states, and so on), automatically guessing whether to shift the keyboard to uppercase, and cross-referencing information (for example, learning which cities match which ZIP codes). Magic Cap interprets handwriting as ink and doesn't try to translate it into text.

Magic Cap Is for Communication

Magic Cap is a software platform designed specifically for communication, as shown in this classic message that helped inspire the Magic Cap team. In the spring of 1990, Bill Atkinson received this electronic postcard from his young daughter, Laura, who used an early software prototype to convey her thoughts simply and creatively, and her dad was able to read and enjoy her message at his convenience (see Figure P-2). This is what Magic Cap does best: personal communication.

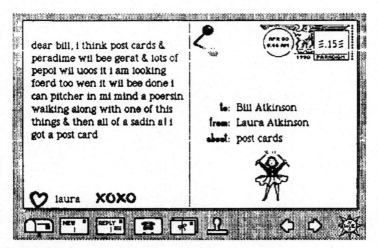

FIGURE P-2. "A ! I got a postcard"

About This Book

By the time you read this book, you may already have a Magic Cap communicator, or not. You don't need to have a communicator for the book to be useful. If you have one, you can use this book as a complementary tutorial, and you might use the examples as a springboard for your own ideas. If you don't have a communicator yet, this book shows what Magic Cap can do and how you might be able to use it.

This book explains the concepts of Magic Cap and shows some practical examples of its use. Many of the scenarios are completely realistic and can be accomplished with the first Magic Cap communicators. You may find yourself using your communicator in exactly the same way, with only the names changed. Some other examples show how Magic Cap might develop over time, a kind of wishful thinking that could happen if communicators become popular. This book is pretty specific in stating what Magic Cap can do now, and what it might do in the future.

Magic Cap software was substantially done before this book was written, but some small details may have changed since then.

Acknowledgments

I didn't realize how many people were vitally important in publishing a book until I wrote one.

Everyone I worked with at Addison-Wesley was wonderful, even the people I never met who were responsible for the cover and art design. Martha Steffen was extremely helpful in explaining the publishing process, negotiating a breakneck schedule, suggesting ways to improve the manuscript, and calming down a nervous author. Every author should have an editor like Martha.

Joanne Clapp Fullagar managed all the production details so smoothly and completely from both coasts that the schedule seemed hectic but not impossible. I really appreciated her encouragement and suggestions.

Keith Wollman and Steve Stansel took a chance on publishing a book by an unproven writer about software still being written.

Tema Goodwin provided thorough and thoughtful copyediting that considerably improved the book.

Bill Fallon and Bob Garnet from AT&T reviewed parts of the manuscript, offering their suggestions and insight.

The folks at General Magic were encouraging and helpful. Curtis Sasaki and Jane Anderson helped get the project started, and Joanna Hoffman gave continuing support. Along with Curtis, Lynn Franklin, Susan Rayl, Terry Moody, Kevin Lynch, and John Sullivan also reviewed the manuscript to make sure I got things right.

David Hendler, a most literate writer, is also reviewing the book.

Bill Atkinson and Laura Atkinson gave me permission to reprint the wonderful postcard Laura sent to her dad. Bill also let me borrow his extensive collection of postcards sent and received in early 1990 to give me an excellent perspective on the evolution of Magic Cap.

The Magic Cap engineers offered their encouragement, and I thank them for answering all of my questions about how things worked (or didn't) and why they worked that way (or didn't). I am grateful to them for letting me share the magic.

My family, as always, was very supportive. Helen Schulman kept telling me that she always knew I would write a book someday, and I'm glad I could prove her right. Thanks, Mom.

Gene Schulman kept asking how the book was coming while he reminded me to take care of myself, and I know he is a very proud father right now. Thanks, Dad.

Louis and Jennifer Schulman came for a visit right in the middle of this frenzy. That weekend helped me keep my sanity.

Jess Knaster was very understanding about not getting to go anywhere for several weekends in a row because of "Mom's book." He waited as patiently as an eight-year-old can wait for his parents to take a break from work to play with him. He even let me use him in some examples in the book. Thanks, Jess. You're a great kid.

Scott Knaster was (and still is) my inspiration. He was the technical reviewer of this book, and he helped create all the figures. He was also the source of the General Magic anecdotes. He micro-scheduled every page sc this book could be finished in an amazingly short time, and he worked beside me on many late nights making this book better. He told me I could do it and then helped me actually do it. I'm so lucky to be married to my best friend.

Chapter 1

✵ Getting Started

The First Time

You're probably interested in personal communicators because you've always been one of the first to get your hands on the newest technology—the industry calls you an *early adopter*, or a *heat-seeker*. Maybe your boss suggested that using one while you're traveling is good business, or you have an incredibly understanding spouse who bought you one for your birthday. On the other hand, maybe you haven't decided to take the plunge yet, but you want to know what it feels like to have one. Whatever the circumstance, you've joined the brave new world of personal communicators.

The first few minutes with a communicator are among the most important in your relationship, kind of like the experience between nervous job applicant and thorough interviewer. When you take it out of the box and start using it, you should feel good about the experience, not uncomfortable. You shouldn't feel overwhelmed by incomprehensible setup procedures or three different thick manuals, each of which says "read me first." General Magic and its alliance partners worked hard to make your beginning experiences pleasant, friendly, and reassuring. In this chapter, we'll go through the process of unpacking and setting up a new Magic Cap communicator.

Basics

Although Magic Cap communicators come in various models from several different manufacturers, they all have many features in common. Most important is that all Magic Cap communicators are operated by touching pictures of objects on the screen. You don't have to use lots of different gestures when touching the screen to make things happen. There are really just two actions you have to learn: touch and slide. To touch, just place your finger or stylus on an object, and then let go. To slide, touch any object and move it along the screen, as if you were sliding it aside. Everything in Magic Cap operates with those two actions.

To help you figure out what you're doing, Magic Cap creates a little world inside your communicator. This world is filled with familiar objects, such as a desk, a telephone, a datebook, an in box, and a clock. To learn to use Magic Cap, you start with what you already know about working with these and other familiar objects.

When you look at a Magic Cap communicator, you'll see that it comes with just one physical key, labeled *option*. If you hold down the option key while touching certain objects on the screen, you can make an alternate or advanced action take place. These optional movements are often used to take advantage of shortcuts for actions—they're never used for common or required functions.

Every Magic Cap communicator has a jack where you can plug in a telephone line. This is how you'll use your communicator to send and receive electronic mail, make phone calls, and send faxes. Some communicators also have built-in two-way data radios for sending and receiving information without having to connect a phone line.

Getting Started

Your first step should be installing the batteries in your communicator. Putting them in at the factory would drain some of their power during shipping and shelf time, so you get to have fresh batteries by installing them yourself. Every communicator has at least three sources of power: a main battery, a backup battery, and a wall adapter. Power is vitally important to your communicator—if it ever loses power completely, it will lose the information you entered! Magic Cap has an elaborate warning system to tell you when your main and backup batteries are running down.

Once you've installed the batteries, the next step is to turn on your communicator. The first images you'll see are the logo of the manufacturer and the Magic Cap rabbit-in-the-hat logo, and the provocative instruction to *Touch the screen to begin*. Your first action will be to teach the communicator about how hard your touch is and to fine-tune the screen's alignment. Magic Cap puts a bull's-eye target in the upper-left corner and asks you to touch it. When you touch it, the communicator's speaker sounds an approving *pop* and the target hops around to two other locations on the screen, calibrating your touch so that it will be more responsive to it.

While you're aligning the touch screen by tapping the targets, you're subtly experiencing three of the key elements of using Magic Cap. First, almost everything is accomplished by touching pictures you see on the screen. Second, when something changes its location on the screen, you'll usually see animation that makes it move rather than just having to figure out that it's gone from one place to another. This animation reinforces what you're seeing so that you're not surprised when the item appears in a new location.

Third, the targets make a popping sound when you touch them. In Magic Cap, most actions make sounds. As you get familiar with Magic Cap, these sounds will become reassuring and will help you confirm your actions. Of course, if you find the sounds annoying or you don't want to disturb people nearby, you can change them or turn them off completely.

Just a Touch. Magic Cap communicators come with a stylus, a sort of pen with no ink, but Magic Cap's hardware and software were designed to let you use your finger if you prefer. The stylus is required for only two functions: the alignment targets, since they need to be touched as precisely as possible to set the screen, and for handwriting, which is really tough to do well with your finger. You can do everything else with a stylus or your finger.

Magic Cap tries to be generous in deciding where you can touch things to activate them. Some items have an invisible halo around them so you can actually miss them by just a little when you use your fingertip to touch or slide. Some items require more precision, such as when you're typing on the keyboard; you can use your fingernail to get a better shot at them. As you use your communicator, you'll have a better idea of whether you want to use your finger or a stylus.

Magic Cap's manuals and information windows use two different words, *tap* and *touch*, to describe the action of placing your finger on an item on the screen and then removing your finger. Although *tap* is more appropriate for a button and *touch* is often used with other kinds of objects, the terms are completely interchangeable, and this book follows suit.

After you finish target practice, you get your first look at the desk and you see your first information window, as shown in Figure 1-1. The window suggests that you touch its *Getting Started* button to set up your communicator, but if you're not ready for that, you can touch the *x* in the upper-right corner of the window to close it and postpone the *Getting Started* stuff.

FIGURE 1-1. The desk with its information window open

You can always go back to *Getting Started* when you're ready by touching the circled question mark next to the word *Desk* in the upper-left corner of the screen, then tapping *Getting Started* in the window that appears. In fact, you can get information about any screen or window by touching that circled question mark. It's a good idea to run through *Getting Started* as the first thing you do with your new communicator.

There are three kinds of actions in the *Getting Started* process. First, there are vital setup tasks you must do to personalize your communicator before you can do almost anything useful. The second kind are actions that you should do before proceeding but that aren't absolutely required. Third, there are instructive lessons that teach skills you might pick up on your own as you're using Magic Cap but that help cut down on any apprehension you might feel when you begin.

Starting the Lessons

There are two things you must do to personalize your communicator before getting much of anything done: You have to tell it who you are and where you are. *Getting Started* provides lessons that help you enter this important information. When you enter your name and location, it's important to recognize that these are not just practice examples; the information you give is saved and should be the real stuff.

What happens if you try to skip ahead and avoid entering your name or location before continuing? Many functions work fine whether they know your name or not: You can use the calculator, write in the notebook, or play a game without filling in your name. If you try to write a message, though, Magic Cap will gently remind you to enter your name first (it even says *please*).

Doing the Time Warp. During Magic Cap's testing, many users thought that *Getting Started* was just a teaching tour of Magic Cap that let them practice doing things, not realizing that setup information entered there was very real. This led to lots of communicators being set up by people named Frank N. Furter and Bugs Bunny. Be sure to type the real information when you go through *Getting Started*.

If you touch *Getting Started*, instructions will lead you into the hallway, then down to the library where the *Getting Started* book waits for you. You'll be directed to tap the *Getting Started* book, as pictured in Figure 1-2, and you'll see the opening pages of the book.

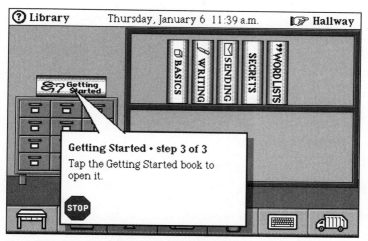

FIGURE 1-2. Just about to open the *Getting Started* book

When you start a lesson, you'll see the number of steps you'll need to follow to complete the lesson, and you'll know many you've done so far. The steps also tell you exactly what you're supposed to do and why, rather than just doing it for you. When a lesson step tells you to tap something, the step's window has a tail pointing to the item so you really get the idea behind the action as well as its consequences.

The first lesson is about the book itself, explaining each feature and action that you can expect. It introduces the buttons that you'll use to move from one step to another and the stop sign that all steps have in case you want to quit the lesson. If you stop a lesson, you will go back to where you started. Even if you stop, you can complete the lesson at any time; in fact, when you go back to the library, the *Getting Started* book even remembers what page you were on.

The next four lessons are about general user features like the top and bottom of the screen and the keyboard. You can finish these lessons sequentially, which will help you feel more comfortable using your communicator by the time you reach the vital lessons that you must complete. If you want, you can skip directly to the lesson about what you must do to personalize your communicator—making a name for yourself.

Required Setup

Before you can make an appointment, create a message, or register for a mail service, the communicator needs to know who you are. There are nine steps to this process, but four of them are navigation steps that take you from place to place, and one step is just an explanation of what you're about to do, so it's easier than it sounds.

If you follow the lessons in order, you'll know about typing by the time you get to the lesson that helps you enter your name. You'll know that the on-screen keyboard appears on the screen when you need to type in some information, and that Magic Cap shows where you're going to type when you need to enter your name, address, and phone number. You may notice that some of your entries are finished automatically, because Magic Cap knows some words and tries to guess what you want to enter so you don't have to type as much. If Magic Cap guesses wrong or you don't even notice that it has guessed, you can continue to type without having to do anything else—your typing will replace Magic Cap's guess. You can find out more about this automatic word-completion feature in Chapter 5.

As soon as you touch the *done* button after filling in your name, Magic Cap puts up an announcement telling you that it's personalizing the communicator for you and that it may take a couple of minutes. You'll also see a spinning hat, which tells you that the communicator is actually busy thinking, not just waiting for you to do something.

Spinning Its Wheels.   When Magic Cap personalizes your communicator, it often takes a couple of minutes. What on earth is it doing all that time? It's calculating a security code that will be used to prove that you're who you say you are when you communicate with other people and services. It takes so long because it's a very big number that's undergoing a lot of calculating, and Magic Cap communicators were designed to be great communicators, not super-fast number-crunching monsters. The good news is that it only has to do this calculation once when you set up your communicator.

Next you'll be directed to fill in your address, and then your phone number. You don't even have to put the parentheses around the area code or the hyphen after the first three numbers; it will take care of that for you. However, you do need to enter your area code. If you don't, Magic Cap will make an upset noise, insert the empty parentheses before your phone number, and place the typing point there for you.

Magic Cap's designers knew that an undersize on-screen keyboard is not the world's easiest way to enter information, so they made sure that Magic Cap is engaged in a never-ending battle to help you enter information more quickly. For example, when you're asked to fill in your address, Magic Cap guesses that your address starts with a number, so it sets the keyboard to its number mode automatically. If your address is a post office box, or something else that begins with a letter, you can easily switch it back to see the standard keyboard.

In addition, the keyboard also makes smart guesses about capitalization. After you've typed the numbers, the keyboard not only switches back to showing letters, but it also shifts to uppercase for you. After you type the first letter, the shift is removed and the letters are lowercase again.

Before you can send a message or even make a phone call, there is one more must-do task: You have to tell the communicator where you're calling from so it knows whether to include area codes and country codes when dialing numbers. You should definitely follow the *Getting Started* lesson for this one, because it's not the most intuitive process in Magic Cap.

Set up dialing is the way to tell Magic Cap about the places you expect to be when you connect a phone line. Your communicator can feel when you plug in a phone line, and it will ask your location every time it gets connected. Phone numbers must be dialed differently depending on where you are; for example, when you dial your home number from outside your own area, you must dial the area code first; when you call from inside your own area, dialing your own area code first will prevent the call from going through.

Again, don't let the number of steps fool you—four of the seven steps are just navigation to get to and from the *Getting Started* book. While you're setting up the dialing locations, you'll get to see the stamper, which is one of the buttons that's always available on the bottom of the screen. You'll learn that the stamper contains lots of rubber stamps that you can use throughout Magic Cap, plus special-use stamps like the ones that fill out name cards and locations.

The standard stamps for locations are *home*, *work*, and *hotel*, but each stamp lets you customize the name, so you can have more than one office, add more hotels as you travel, or come up with other locations. When you set up your dialing location, you'll be asked to choose a stamp that matches your actual location.

After typing the name of your location, you'll enter your country, area code, and whether you need to dial a prefix to get an outside line first. If you've already filled out your name card with a phone number, Magic Cap will guess that you're in that number's area code, an example of Magic Cap's smart integration. You can read more about this phone location business in Chapter 6.

After you touch *done*, you will have completed the only two tasks required to start using Magic Cap. Every other lesson is just enhancement and teaching, but you'll probably want to complete most of them anyway.

If these two setup tasks are so important, why aren't they the first lessons in *Getting Started*? Before Magic Cap lets you complete these setup lessons, it teaches you how to use the skills you'll need to do them. It wants to make sure you know how to type, use the stamper, and navigate from place to place before asking you to do real work with those skills.

More Setting Up

After you finish the two required lessons, setting the time and date is a good lesson to go through next. Your communicator will let you do everything it can do without making you set the time and date, but it won't be very accurate. For example, it wouldn't be very useful to have an appointment set to the wrong date or to send mail that has the wrong time in its postmark.

You can turn the pages in the *Getting Started* book until you find the lesson entitled *Set the time and date*. Once again, the 15 steps listed make it sound tedious, but 4 are for moving around in Magic Cap, and each time you set a number or time zone, touching the *accept* button to move on counts as a step as well, so it'll seem much easier than that. Figure 1-3 shows the first step in the lesson that sets the time and date.

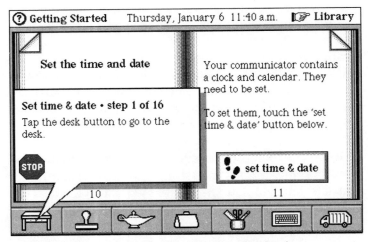

FIGURE 1-3. Starting to set the clock and calendar

As with some other lessons, the first thing you need to do is go back to the desk by touching the desk image on the bottom of your screen. By touching the clock behind the desk, it zooms up close enough for you to set it. The first thing you're asked to do is select a city in your time zone. Magic Cap wants to know this so it can adjust the

12

clock if you go to other cities. Your exact location may not show up in the list of cities you can choose from, so you can select any city that's in the same time zone. After the communicator knows what time zone it's in, it asks you to tell it what time it is.

After you set the time, you get to set the calendar to today's date. To set the date, you'll see a calendar page that lets you choose the year, month, and date. You'll use left and right arrows to help you move forward and backward in time. You finish up the lesson in the same way you've finished other lessons—you go back to the *Getting Started* book and tap *done*. Your communicator has learned a lot today; it knows who you are, where you're calling from, and the date and time.

The next lesson to go through signs you up for AT&T's PersonaLink service. This is another one that you should do, but you might choose to skip. As with all the others, you can either step through it with the help of the lesson, try its task yourself, or skip it altogether. This one is pretty straightforward, so if you're feeling really comfortable with your communicator, you might want to try flying solo on this one, going without the lesson. The only prerequisite is that you should be connected to a phone line to complete this process.

When you turn on your communicator, you'll find one or more messages in the in box above the desk—the exact number and the messages vary depending on which communicator you have. Some of these messages are offers from information networks to provide electronic mail and other services for your communicator, including one from AT&T.

When you tap an offer message to open it, you'll see that it has a button to request the signup materials from the service. If you're connected to a phone line, tap the button; the request will be answered with a return message that includes the rest of the registration materials. Taking this lesson not only helps you register for a mail service that will give you a much more powerful communicator, it also helps you successfully and easily send your first message.

Lessons that Teach

We have now covered what you must do and what you should do to effectively and efficiently set up your new communicator. The other lessons found in the *Getting Started* book are more instructive than task-oriented: They teach you about the top and bottom of the screen and how to use the keyboard. By going through them, you'll have a better understanding of Magic Cap, its tools and commands, the places you can go in Magic Cap, and what you'll be able to do with your communicator.

The lesson about the top of the screen is short and sweet. It points out the areas along the top of the screen and describes each one. You'll learn that the top of the screen tells you where you are in the Magic Cap world, what the date is, and how much battery power you have remaining.

The lesson about the bottom of the screen is more detailed, pointing out the commands and tools that are available throughout Magic Cap. As each button is presented, it appears in its place along the bottom of the screen. The lesson describes each button in general terms: the desk button, the stamper, the lamp, the tote bag, the tool holder, the keyboard button, and the garbage truck. You can find out about all these things as you're working, but the lessons are like a shortcut to knowing how to use Magic Cap more effectively.

Making the Scene. The space between the top and bottom of the screen is called the current *scene*. Common scenes include the desk, items on the desk such as the name file or a notebook page, the hallway and rooms in the hallway, the street downtown, or buildings on the street. For example, when you open the name file, a name card fills the screen; that's the name card scene. When you want to set the clock, you touch it and it zooms up close so that you can see it and nothing else; that's the clock scene. When you want to write a message, you touch the postcard at the center of the desk. This is like pulling the new card up so close that you actually see only the postcard scene. Magic Cap also includes windows, which are rectangles that float above the scene and are filled with items to help you perform actions or enter information. There's more about this stuff in Chapter 3.

The keyboard lesson has the most steps, but if you're going to be typing lots of information, the lesson is a few minutes' time well spent. As the keyboard opens, the lesson describes all the features built into the keyboard as it leads you step by step in typing a few words. You'll learn about the keyboard's smart capitalization and the switch that lets you change the keyboard from letters to numbers and symbols. The lesson also tells you about the typing point, the vertical line that shows Magic Cap where you want to begin typing.

The next lesson, *Add your signature,* is kind of fun to complete. You'll get a better feel for using the stylus as a writing tool on the screen as you sign your name. If you don't do this lesson right away, you can always add your signature at another time. Once you've completed this lesson, you'll find stamps with your signature on them in the stamper when you're writing a message.

If you haven't added your signature but you decide you really want to sign your name on a message you're writing, you'll find empty signature stamps in the stamper. When you drop one of these stamps on your message, you'll go directly to the signature entry form, where you can sign on the dotted line. If you decide later that you're not happy with your signature, you can always repeat the lesson to change it.

 Clip 'n' Save.   Sometimes Magic Cap has to provide a visual representation of things that don't have a real physical metaphor, such as a few words of text or a particular style of shadow for an item on the screen. For such situations, Magic Cap provides coupons, complete with dotted-line borders, that represent those intangible things. For example, a coupon that represents a shadow style is good for one shadow in that style; you just drop it on an item and the item gets the new shadow. Before you sign your name, the signature stamps are really coupons that are redeemable for one stamp with your signature. When you put one on a message, Magic Cap will ask you to sign your name.

The last two teaching lessons in *Getting Started* actually step you through sequences that demonstrate the heart of Magic Cap, communication. One lesson helps you make a phone call to someone, and the other walks through the steps necessary to send a message. Once you're registered for the AT&T service, you can send a message to someone. You can use the phone lesson right away.

When you do the *Phone someone you know* lesson, you will be able to hear the call being dialed through the speaker in your communicator, but you'll have to use a handset or telephone to talk. After you've entered the phone number from the Magic Cap keypad, you can touch *dial* to have your communicator call for you. You'll get a *Phone status* window that lets you adjust the volume, and you'll see a timer that shows the duration of the call.

You can have a person-to-person conversation through the standard telephone, and then use the communicator to hang up. To complete the lesson, you can save the phone number by making a new name card for the person you called so you'll have the number handy the next time you want to call. Touch *done*, and you're back in the library ready to go on.

The last page of *Getting Started* congratulates you for finishing the lessons. If you tap *put away*, the book closes and hops back onto the shelf until you need to read it again. When you reach the end of *Getting Started*, you have finished setting up your communicator. You have also made a name card, used the phone, sent a message, written your name, and learned all the skills you'll need to get the most out of your communicator.

Lessons Learned

When you finish each lesson, the text on that page of the book is updated to reflect the completion of the series of steps, and the button changes to *repeat lesson*, which you can do whenever you want. After you finish the lesson, you will also get directions on what to do next.

The lessons try hard to protect you from straying and doing anything else that might cause unnecessary frustration. If you touch the wrong item at any lesson step, you'll hear a gentle reminder sound and see the proper location blinking on the screen. If you don't finish the required lessons, you can always complete the tasks on your own if you're the kind of person who learns best by experimenting, rather than by following a preset sequence.

Remember that if you don't complete the lessons, and you don't finish the setup manually, you won't be able to do most substantive tasks. When you try, a window appears and reminds you to personalize your communicator with your name or location; it even includes a button for returning you to the lesson with a single touch. And it says *please*.

The *Getting Started* book shows you how to use many of the tools and features available in your communicator and helps you set up vital information like your name and location. After completing the lessons, you'll feel more comfortable with the way Magic Cap works. Most important, if you've completed the *Getting Started* book, you've learned how to use your communicator for what it does best—communicate!

Chapter 2

 ## Electronic Mail

Keep in Touch

Using technology to keep in touch used to mean picking up the phone, speaking to an operator, and asking her (yes, it was always her) to ring Grandpa Dave's house. As more people got telephones and the technology moved forward, customers felt more comfortable with phone numbers that looked like FLorida 5-2379 or KEystone 7-9855. Amazing advances let people use a telephone in their home to call someone in another city, or state, or even country. Telephones in public places worked by depositing coins, helping people stay in touch without having to stay at home.

Now, technology offers services that the venerable Alexander Graham Bell probably couldn't have imagined. We have phones that work without wires, giving you the freedom to call from your car, on a camping trip, or over the Rocky Mountains (although a lot of those conversations probably consist of "That's right—I'm calling from the airplane!").

As people became more mobile and used phones while they were away from home, they started to worry more that while they were away, someone might be calling them. Answering machines and voice mail were at first considered unacceptably rude—I used to think that if I wanted to call my friend, she should at least have the decency to stay home and wait for my call, and I never liked leaving a message. Now many people consider it poor etiquette not to have voice mail or an answering machine, as an unanswered telephone inconveniences the caller.

Many people who resisted answering machines ultimately recognized that they give you freedom as both a caller and a receiver of calls. As a caller, you can fulfill your urge to communicate even if you can't reach anyone. When you're called, you can miss the call without missing its content.

This is the foundation of Magic Cap: power, flexibility, and convenience for the sender and the receiver. I want to communicate with you right now, but you may not be willing or able to hear from me right now. I can tell you what I need and go back to the rest of my life. You're free to get my communication at your convenience. Magic Cap expands this communication to cover electronic mail that contains digital information like words, pictures, sounds, cartoons, appointments, sketches, and more, along with the more-familiar phone calls and faxes.

This chapter covers four important scenes in Magic Cap: the in box, the out box, the AT&T building, and most important, the message-writing scene, which is where all new messages are created.

Communication at Heart

There are several elements at the heart of a Magic Cap communicator. The core of Magic Cap's communication features is the built-in Telescript language. While Telescript is transparent to you as a user, its communication features help Magic Cap deliver electronic mail features that you'll use in lots of different ways.

When you get a Magic Cap communicator, you can sign up for an electronic mailbox with one or more services. In fact, AT&T has built a brand-new network service, AT&T PersonaLink Services, that is based on Telescript. Sending and receiving electronic mail is one of PersonaLink's key features.

Lots of people already have electronic mailboxes with other, existing services and networks, such as America Online, CompuServe, and Internet. Magic Cap lets you communicate with most of these existing services, even if you don't have mailboxes on those systems. It's kind of like this: You can use an automated teller machine that belongs to a bank where you don't have an account, as long as your bank has an agreement to talk to the other bank. As long as you're registered with PersonaLink, you can exchange mail with people on lots of other services. This communication between services happens through communication *gateways*.

Any time you enter a different world, which is what happens when you go through a gateway, you have to play by the rules of the new world. Sometimes, stuff gets left at the door and you can only send in what the other service can understand. For example, most electronic mail services don't know how to have pictures or sounds in their messages, so if you include those items in your messages, they probably won't get delivered to recipients on other services. Even with these limitations, being able to send mail to someone on another service without having to subscribe to it is very useful.

Some of the conventional mail services provide special software packages that let you use Magic Cap to connect to them directly. If you have one of these packages, you can use your communicator to talk to the service for mail and other information. Whether you're connected to PersonaLink or a conventional service, you can use Magic Cap to keep in touch with colleagues, family, and friends.

AT&T PersonaLink Services

Just what is PersonaLink? Why should you register for it? How can PersonaLink get in touch with people on other services? That's a lot of questions for some service from New Jersey. Users can send, receive, and store their messages with PersonaLink, and they can also use the gateways that PersonaLink offers to other conventional mail services. Electronic mail is only one feature of PersonaLink. AT&T's network service will take advantage of Telescript's intelligent agents to offer other kinds of communicating packages and information services.

Mostly Cloudy. A Telescript-based service such as PersonaLink consists of one or more computers running one or more Telescript *engines,* or programs that understand Telescript. Engineers often refer to the computers and Telescript engines together as "the cloud." In honor of this nickname, the sky over Magic Cap's downtown always has a puffy cloud floating down the street.

When you first get your communicator, you'll find a message or two waiting in the in box when you turn it on—registration offers for PersonaLink and other services. After you've personalized your communicator with your name and phone number, you'll probably take a look at those messages. You'll find the signup procedure pretty straightforward. Depending on your model of communicator and the service you're signing up for, you might have to make sure you're connected to a phone line first. Then, tap *get signup form* at the bottom of the offer letter. A sample of one of these service offer messages appears in Figure 2-1.

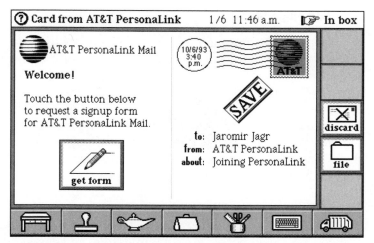

FIGURE 2-1. Request card for PersonaLink signup materials

When you tap the button, Magic Cap sends a message to the mail service requesting a signup form. You see the new message hop to the out box, and then watch a progress bar as the message is sent from your communicator to the service. When your communicator finishes, there's a new message in your in box—the signup form you asked for.

When you reply to the offer (again, you should plug into a phone line if your communicator and the service don't support wireless messages), your name card information is sent to the company providing the service so it can respond by sending you registration materials. If you're not connected to a phone line and you don't have wireless hardware when you respond, the message hops into the out box, waiting to be sent. Then, you can send the message when you connect to a phone line later.

Once you've signed up with a mail service, you can start sending messages right away.

Sending a Message

Because communicating is at the center of Magic Cap, the image of the postcard and pencil is right in the middle of the desk. To start making a new message, you just tap that postcard. There's also a desk drawer that holds a variety of stationery for other kinds of messages.

Magic Cap was designed around whole person thinking, which contends that people don't strictly separate their days into business and personal parts; instead, they weave them together, acting on impulses and needs as they come up. If Magic Cap succeeds, electronic mail will become popular for individuals as well as for businesses. Magic Cap provides clues to this focus. First, the devices are called *personal* communicators, and second, Magic Cap is factory-set to use postcards, not business letters, as the standard form of electronic mail, although you can easily switch to business letters instead.

With that in mind, let's go through a couple of electronic mail scenarios, a personal example and a business example.

Getting Personal

Imagine an old friend, Sheryl, whom you've known since grade school or maybe even kindergarten. Now, even though you live in different states, you still like to keep in touch beyond just birthday and holiday cards. A fact of your lives, though, is that while you might often think about her, it's difficult for you (and for her) to coordinate your time well enough to have a reasonable telephone conversation.

By writing an electronic message, you can jot down all the things you want to tell her about your life and ask her about hers, all while you're waiting for a staff meeting to begin. When you connect to a phone line, you can let her know you've been thinking about her without having to worry about time zone differences. She can read your message and respond when her time is less complicated. Sheryl won't have to try to find a time when you're both home and not busy at the same time. In fact, this even works if she's out of town on business or vacation, because she'll certainly have her communicator with her.

To make the message, touch the postcard, and a new, blank message hops onto the desk and then zooms open to fill the screen. The new message also automatically opens the name chooser, a window that lists everybody in your name file, so you can choose your friend's name from the list (see Figure 2-2). If your friend isn't in your name file yet, you can add a new card for her by tapping *new*—you don't have to go to the name file to add a name. If you're not sure whom to address the message to right now, you can tap the *x* to close the name chooser.

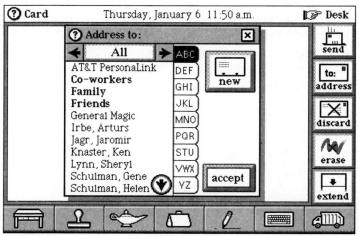

FIGURE 2-2.   New message scene with name chooser

To address the message, touch your friend's name, and then touch *accept* to close the name chooser. You'll see that Sheryl's name has been added to the postcard as the addressee, and your name appears as the sender. You'll also find that Magic Cap has guessed that you'll want to start the message with a standard salutation, so it has typed *Dear Sheryl,* in the upper-left corner of the postcard. Of course, you can change this salutation if you want.

Magic Cap lets you choose between typing (for letter-perfect text) and writing (for drawings or a more personal feel). This is likely to be a fairly long letter, so you will probably want to type most of it. You can touch the keyboard image on the bottom of the screen to open the on-screen keyboard. If you find that you usually prefer to type messages rather than write them, you can customize Magic Cap so that it opens the keyboard instead of selecting a pencil when you make a new message.

When the keyboard opens, you can start typing directly below the salutation, or you can move to any other spot on the postcard where you might want to begin. Because it's been a while since the two of you spoke, you have a lot to tell your friend. After you've typed in your news and asked about her family, you might notice that Magic Cap has automatically enlarged the postcard for you so you can write as much as you need to without worrying about running out of room (see Figure 2-3). You can tell because an arrow pointing up appears when you reach the bottom of the card, but you can still type as if you had unlimited space, which you do. It would be great if paper postcards worked like that—then we wouldn't have to worry about writing so small. In the future, maybe there will be postcards for Magic Cap that have nice pictures on the back and we'll just send those instead.

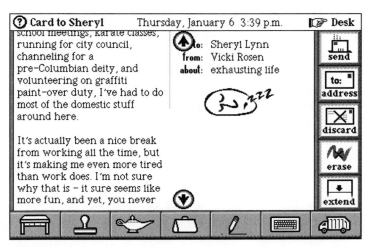

school meetings, karate classes, running for city council, channeling for a pre-Columbian deity, and volunteering on graffiti paint-over duty, I've had to do most of the domestic stuff around here.

It's actually been a nice break from working all the time, but it's making me even more tired than work does. I'm not sure why that is – it sure seems like more fun, and yet, you never

to: Sheryl Lynn
from: Vicki Rosen
about: exhausting life

send
to:
address
discard
erase
extend

FIGURE 2-3. Longer text automatically extends the length of the card

When you're done typing, you can open the stamp drawer so you can stamp your signature and a sleeping face stamp (the theme of your postcard is "I'm working real hard and I'm tired"). If you want, you can touch *about:* to open the keyboard and fill in a description for the postcard, which would let Sheryl know if the card is just general news or if you really need something in particular, like her recipe for pickles.

Mailing the Card

As soon as you addressed the card, a stamp showing how the card will be delivered (that is, whether by fax, PersonaLink, America Online, or whatever) appeared in the upper-right corner. If you want to change the delivery choice, you can tap the stamp and choose another method. Magic Cap knows to list only the delivery choices that will actually work for the recipient; in other words, if your friend doesn't have a CompuServe account, CompuServe isn't listed as a delivery choice. When you've made the right choice, tap *send,* and the postcard zooms down onto the desk and hops into the out box.

If you're connected to a phone line or have wireless access to the delivery choice you selected, Magic Cap will mail the postcard right away. If you can't connect, the mail will wait in the out box. Then, when a phone line is handy, you can open the out box, tap *mail*, and watch the message fly off to Sheryl. The next time she checks her mail, your message will be waiting for her.

Electronic mail has a different feel than a phone call. It's certainly not as interactive, but it can be more thoughtful, and you can communicate and keep in touch without having to find a time when you're both focused and uninterrupted. You get to write a letter with no pen, paper, envelope, stamp, or post office involved; it's delivered very quickly; and your friend gets to read and respond easily and at her convenience.

Replying and Forwarding

Of course, after Sheryl reads the message, you hope she'll want to respond. She can use a built-in shortcut for replying to your message. The command buttons along the right side of your message include choices for *reply* and *forward*. If you look at Figure 2-4, you can see these buttons along with the rest of the card as it looks when Sheryl receives it.

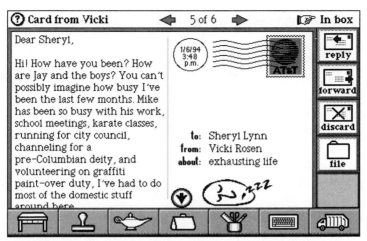

Dear Sheryl,

Hi! How have you been? How are Jay and the boys? You can't possibly imagine how busy I've been the last few months. Mike has been so busy with his work, school meetings, karate classes, running for city council, channeling for a pre-Columbian deity, and volunteering on graffiti paint-over duty, I've had to do most of the domestic stuff around here.

1/6/94
3:48
p.m.

AT&T

to: Sheryl Lynn
from: Vicki Rosen
about: exhausting life

reply

forward

discard

file

FIGURE 2-4. Message has been received and opened

When Sheryl is ready to respond, she can ask Magic Cap to create a new card by tapping *reply*. Because it's a shortcut, *reply* also fills in the address (back to you, the sender), guesses the salutation, opens the keyboard, and positions the typing point. A reply stamp appears at the bottom of the card, and an appropriate delivery choice is selected. Of course, she can change any of this stuff as she writes her reply. The next time you check your mail, her reply is there.

If the message wasn't just gossipy, but really was a request for the pickle recipe, you might also want to forward her reply to your friend Phil. To do that, tap *forward* on the right side of the screen while you're looking at her reply. Tapping *forward* makes a new card, opens the name chooser to let you address it, and attaches a copy of her message with the recipe. Once again, Magic Cap makes a delivery choice based on the information in the name file, and you can change the choice if you want.

Staying In Touch on the Road

One of the most frustrating situations in business is when you're out of your office and you need to communicate with someone else who is also out of the office. Your voice mail systems can have one-sided conversations, but there are times when communication needs to be more substantive and immediate. Electronic mail provides a thoughtful, reflective medium for getting your thoughts down just as you want them, a nice alternative to the ticking clock and live recording of voice mail.

Let's say you're the assistant director for an animation art gallery, and your gallery in Denver is just two days away from the opening of a big show. You're in Chicago, ready to accompany the animation cels from the corporate warehouse to Denver. The gallery director, Helen, is in Los Angeles, ready to accompany the artist on his flight to that show. Neither of you is in your gallery office, and neither of you is very reachable by telephone (just multiply the problems of getting messages from hotel operators by two). This is a job for Magic Cap.

Opening your communicator's desk drawer, you can begin a business letter to send to your boss by touching its image. When you touch the business letter, it hops out of the drawer and onto your desk, automatically opening the name chooser so you can address it to Helen. As with a postcard, you can always just touch the *x* to close the name chooser without picking an addressee right away.

The business letter automatically includes the sender's name in the upper-right corner of the letter (like letterhead), adds today's date, and then the salutation to the addressee, in this case *Dear Helen*. It also opens the keyboard and places the typing point for you. You need to ask her about which art pieces should be sent for the show, as well as what kind of wine and hors d'oeuvres to serve at the opening, and when the artist will be available for interviews with the local press.

Consistent with other pieces of "paper" in Magic Cap, a business letter can be extended if you need more room at the bottom. After you finish your message, you close the keyboard. You can see the completed letter in Figure 2-5. If you've already addressed the letter and you agree with the delivery choice Magic Cap suggests, you can tap *send* to mail the letter.

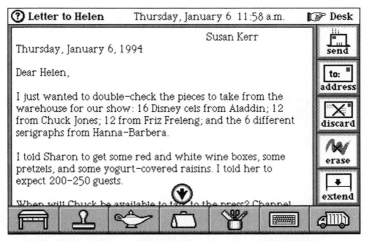

FIGURE 2-5. Business letter automatically adds heading information

Unlike the postcard, where you can see the postage stamp that tells how the message will be delivered, letters put that information on their envelopes. By touching *address* on the right side of the screen, you'll get the standard options to add or replace addressees, and you'll also be able to tap a special button labeled *show envelope*. If you do, you're switched to a different view that resembles the front of an envelope with a company logo in the upper-left corner (see Figure 2-6). You can stamp anything you want on the envelope, or take it off completely by sliding it to the trash.

FIGURE 2-6. Envelope for the business letter

The envelope also has the postage stamp message in the appropriate place in the upper-right corner, and the recipient's name (as well as yours, and an *about:* description) in the center of the envelope. Here's where you can choose how to send your letter. When you communicate with Helen, you usually send a fax because you're typically out of the office while she's at the gallery. This time, you'll use her electronic mail address to send the letter, and you'll also stamp it urgent. You might guess that you should stamp *urgent* on the envelope and not the letter itself, but the urgent stamp will alert Helen's mailbox whether it's on the envelope or on the letter.

After you've switched delivery choices, you can touch *address* again, then *hide envelope* to switch back to the letter. If you're done, you can touch *send* while you're looking at either the letter or the envelope to mail your message. Since Helen has set her in box to alert her when an urgent message comes in, and her communicator has a two-way radio for wireless access to electronic mail, she's able to read your message and respond within minutes. Your mind is eased much more quickly than if you had to wait for her to get back to her hotel, pick up your phone message (if she received it at all) and try to call you back in Chicago. You've helped ensure the success of the big event.

Following the Metaphor.   The differences between Magic Cap letters and postcards are very similar to the differences between actual letters and postcards. Postcards give you a smaller amount of space to write in, your writing isn't hidden inside an envelope, and the addressee's name is printed on the right side of a line that bisects your message. Letters start with a plain piece of paper (although Magic Cap business letters automatically add items you would expect on a business letter), and the address is written on the envelope that holds your message. These are subtle differences, but they're important, especially if you recall Marshall McLuhan's adage about the medium being the message.

Group Therapy

As roads get clogged and gas prices increase, carpools are becoming more popular. Carpools that drive kids to school can be challenging enough to deal with, but for serious hassles, try coordinating a carpool for adults who work in the same office building. Let's see how Magic Cap might help you manage a carpool that takes five people to work each morning.

You're responsible for driving four other people to work one morning each week (because of your varying departure times, you each find another way home at the end of the day). You just found out that you will be out of the office for a week (starting tomorrow) overseeing the beginning of a client's construction project. You need to let the other people know that you'll miss your regular turn driving, as well as not needing a ride the other four days of the week. Everytime something like this comes up, it means trying to catch up with four other busy professionals to rearrange the carpool. You could make four different phone calls, one to each of them, but Magic Cap has a way to let you be more efficient.

Magic Cap helps you handle these kinds of problems by letting you collect name cards together into groups. Any set of names with something in common can form a group. We'll create a group to help manage our carpool. Tap the name file on the desk to open it, tap *new*, then *group*, and then type *Carpool* to name the group. Tap *add* to put people into the group. The result is a filled-out group card, as you can see in Figure 2-7. You can find out more about name cards in Chapter 5.

Now that all the carpool members are reachable on electronic mail or via fax, you can send one message to four people detailing your change in plans.

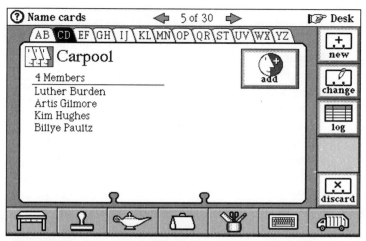

AB CD EF GH IJ KL MN OP QR ST UV WX YZ

🎴 Carpool

add

new

change

log

discard

4 Members
Luther Burden
Artis Gilmore
Kim Hughes
Billye Paultz

FIGURE 2-7. Group name card helps manage multiple addressees

After you tap the postcard to start writing a new message, you can pick *Carpool* as the addressee. The name chooser lists all groups in boldface to make them stand out. You can verify that all the recipients are included in the group by option-tapping *Carpool* in the addressee area, which opens a window listing the members of the group. If you then touch a name in the window, the delivery choice stamp will change to show how the message will be sent to that addressee. Magic Cap lets you have a different delivery choice for each member of a group.

When you tap *send*, the message will go to each member of the group using the delivery choice that Magic Cap guessed was right, or that you corrected. In this case, two copies will go by PersonaLink, one by America Online via a PersonaLink gateway, and one to a work fax number. There are four addressees and three different delivery choices, but you only have to send one message.

☞ Testing Patience. The General Magic team ran into an unexpected and embarrassing problem while testing PersonaLink. A General Magic tester plugged a communicator into a phone line that didn't go through General Magic's switchboard, but mistakenly instructed the communicator to dial 9 for an outside line before calling any numbers. When the communicator called AT&T's access number, which begins with 1-800, it actually started by dialing 9-1-800. Naturally, the telephone network responded with a message to "please dial a 1," determining that the communicator was calling a long distance number in area code 918.

The diligent tester took the message at its word. Thinking that Magic Cap had somehow forgotten to dial the initial 1, the tester cleverly told Magic Cap to dial a 9 for an outside line, then a 1, and then AT&T's number. The next time the communicator tried calling AT&T, it dialed the extraneous 9, then an equally inappropriate 1, followed by the proper 1-800 number. That makes 9-1-1, then 800 and the rest of the number. The PersonaLink service didn't answer, so the tester tried again a few times.

When the police officers and firefighters arrived, they were stern but understanding.

Choosing How Messages Are Delivered

Let's look at the many ways you can send a message. When you create a new message and address it to someone in your name file, Magic Cap puts a postage stamp in the upper-right corner of the message. The postage stamp shows how the message will be delivered to the addressee. That information is called the *delivery choice.* If you've entered delivery information on the addressee's name card, such as a fax number or electronic mail address, the postage stamp shows one of the ways that you can get a message to the addressee.

If an addressee has more than one way to get mail, you can tap the postage stamp to see a choice box that lists the addressee's delivery choices. This works for multiple addressees, too; you can touch the name of an individual addressee to set the delivery choice for just that addressee. As you touch each addressee's name in turn, the postage stamp changes to show the delivery choice for that addressee.

How does Magic Cap decide which delivery choices to offer for a particular addressee? The easy answer is this: It offers all the valid ways of getting the message from you to the addressee. The full answer is more complex. To learn all the valid ways of sending the message, Magic Cap must consider which services you belong to and which services the addressee belongs to. For example, if the addressee has a Prodigy account, Prodigy will appear as a delivery choice only if you have some way of getting mail to Prodigy, either with your own Prodigy account or a gateway to Prodigy from a service you belong to.

So, when building the list of delivery choices, Magic Cap compares the services that you and the addressee belong to, also considering gateways that might get a message flowing between the two of you. But wait, there's more. If the addressee has any fax numbers, they're always listed as delivery choices, because every Magic Cap communicator can send faxes.

Finally, Magic Cap checks to see if you belong to any electronic mail services that know how to look up their members' addresses. Given an addressee's name, these services can check to see if the addressee has a mailbox with them. This feature in an electronic mail service is called *directory lookup*. If you belong to any services that have directory lookup, Magic Cap will add those services to the list of delivery choices for all addressees. PersonaLink is an example of a service that does directory lookup, so once you're registered for PersonaLink, it will appear as a delivery choice every time you address a message.

Here's a summary of how Magic Cap makes its list of delivery choices:

1. Magic Cap checks your name card and the addressee's name card to see if there are any services that you both belong to. If so, those services are added to the list of delivery choices. For example, if you're both CompuServe members, *CompuServe* becomes a delivery choice.

2. Magic Cap checks your name card and the addressee's name card to see if any gateways offered by services you belong to can communicate with any gateways or services that the addressee belongs to. If so, those choices are valid too. For example, if you have an Internet account and the addressee has an MCI Mail account, Magic Cap can determine that MCI Mail has an Internet gateway, so *MCI Mail via Internet* will be added to the list of delivery choices.

3. Magic Cap checks the addressee's name card for any fax numbers. They're added to the list of delivery choices.

4. Magic Cap checks your name card to see if you belong to any services that offer directory lookup. If so, those services are added to the list of delivery choices. For example, if you're a PersonaLink member,

PersonaLink (trying directory) will be added to the list of delivery choices for this and every other addressee.

If you know that an addressee belongs to a particular service, but you don't have the addressee's account number, you can send a message to that addressee only if the service offers directory lookup. PersonaLink's directory lookup feature is particularly powerful and provides several advanced features.

If you're registered with PersonaLink and you want to send a message to your cousin Arturs Irbe, who is also on PersonaLink, you can send the message and ask PersonaLink to look him up. When you address the message, you can tap the postage stamp and pick the *PersonaLink (trying directory)* delivery choice. As detailed, the delivery choices will also include any services that can get mail from you to him, including his fax numbers.

Because you picked the *PersonaLink (trying directory)* stamp, the message will be delivered to the big PersonaLink cloud in the sky. PersonaLink looks for any members it has who are named Arturs Irbe. It even looks phonetically, in case you're a bad Latvian speller. If PersonaLink finds nobody who matches, you'll get an electronic *return to sender* message back from PersonaLink. If there's exactly one person with that name, PersonaLink will go ahead and deliver the message, and also send you a new and improved name card with his account number.

If PersonaLink finds more than one match, which certainly could happen, PersonaLink returns the message to you along with a list of the matching names it found, including additional information like area codes to help identify the correct person. Because cousin Arturs lives in San Jose, the person with the 408 area code is most likely to be him. After you decide which one is right, you can resend the message to him and Magic Cap automatically updates your name file. Hey, this is even better than calling directory assistance.

You don't have to send a message to someone in order to have PersonaLink look them up. You can also go downtown to the PersonaLink building and get a directory lookup form there. Fill out the information as completely as you can and send it in to PersonaLink. If there's a match, PersonaLink will send you the name card. Figure 2-8 shows a directory lookup form.

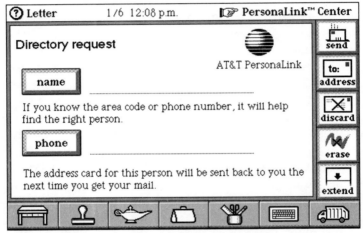

FIGURE 2-8. PersonaLink directory lookup form

Fax and Beam

Although the folks at General Magic and AT&T probably wish it weren't so, it will probably take a short while before you can reach everyone you know on electronic mail. Until then, you'll sometimes have to factor in more traditional means of communication. Most offices, plenty of homes, and even a few cars have fax machines. Your communicator can easily send messages via fax. If you're telecommuting and you need to send something to the office, faxing it might be the easiest and fastest way to get it there.

If it's just a short message, write a postcard or letter and address it to the office fax machine. This is a good excuse for you to enter a name card for your office. Your office's fax number entered there will show up as a delivery choice, and your communicator will send the message just as if it were full-fledged electronic mail. You'll also find a fax command always available inside the lamp. If you sketch a floor plan in the notebook and want to send it to your architect for her advice, you don't have to attach it to a letter. Just tap the lamp, then fax, and you'll see the fax window, which lets you choose exactly what to send, who to send it to, and whether you want to include a cover page. When you're ready, tap *send fax* to deliver your sketch to the architect's fax machine. Figure 2-9 shows the *fax* window.

Magic Cap offers another way to send information that's fast and cheap: infrared beaming. Every Magic Cap communicator has an infrared transmitter and receiver that you can use to send messages, notebook pages, name cards, and other items. Of course, you have to be within a few feet of your recipient's communicator, but that's how infrared technology works.

To send via infrared beam, tap the lamp to open it, then tap *beam*. You'll get a list of what you can send and who you can send it to, as your communicator locates all recipients who are in range. Tap *send* to beam your information.

FIGURE 2-9. Fax is available everywhere in Magic Cap

Customizing for New Messages

When you make a new message, Magic Cap opens the name chooser and asks you to address the new message as it zooms open. If you don't want to address the message right away, you can touch the *x* to close the name chooser and address the message later. If you never want to address messages as soon as they're created, you can ask Magic Cap not to show the name chooser when you make a new message. To do this, tap the lamp, then *rules*, then tap rule 1, *Address new messages right after creating them.* to turn it off.

Every kind of stationery can be set to choose a particular tool when you create a new message on that kind of paper. For example, when you create a new postcard, Magic Cap chooses the thin pencil tool. If you want to change this behavior, you can set a rule to choose a particular tool, such as the thick pencil, when you create a new postcard. If you prefer to type your postcards, you can turn the rule off.

When you're addressing a message, you might want to change the addressee, or add another addressee. When you tap the *address* button on the right side of the screen, you can add a new addressee to those already listed, or you can replace the entire list (see Figure 2-10). If you tap *replace addressees*, the name chooser appears and you can pick a new addressee.

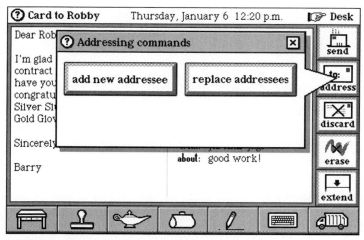

FIGURE 2-10. Addressing commands window

If you want to send a message to multiple addressees, you can tap *add new addressee* and pick from the name chooser. If you want to add more than one addressee at a time, here's a shortcut: Touch a name, and then option-touch *accept* to add that name as an addressee and still leave the name chooser open to add more names.

The name chooser also includes a choice box that lets you pick different addressee types. Choices include the standard *to:*; *cc:* for carbon copy (and it's amazing that this term is still around, since nobody actually makes carbon copies anymore); *bcc:* for blind carbon copy, when you want to send a message to someone without showing that it's going to that addressee; and *reply to;* which lets you specify someone else to receive replies to the message. If you're sending a letter rather than a postcard, the *Addressing commands* window also provides a button that lets you see the envelope and hide it once you've opened it.

Just because the plain postcard is located in the middle of your desk doesn't mean you have to use it every time. It's often appropriate for a quick message or a personal note, but if you're sending a business letter, you'll probably want to use more formal stationery. A postcard has the written message out in the open on the left side of the card, and the addressing information on the right side, just like a real postcard. If you tap the drawer on the left side of the desk, you'll find stationery inside. The letters, both plain and business, come with envelopes. The envelopes carry addressing information, a postage stamp, and a postmark. Letters and postcards look different in your in box, but when each is opened, its message appears. Take a look at Figure 2-11 to see what's in the stationery drawer.

When you make a new business letter, Magic Cap prints your name at the top of the page; it then adds the date, the name and address of the addressee, and the salutation, and also opens the keyboard. If you option-tap the business or plain letter, you can edit the stationery itself, not just a sheet of it. You can change the information you want to appear automatically when you make a new letter. For example, if you're sending a business letter, you might want to use your company's name rather than your own.

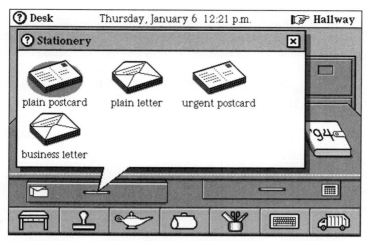

FIGURE 2-11. Different kinds of stationery in the desk drawer

When you option-touch *business letter*, you can see where it auto-types the sender name. If you change that to your company's name, every time you send a business letter, it will appear to be from your company. You can also edit the other information it automatically types, if you want.

To send a personal letter, you can touch *plain letter* in the stationery drawer. It's the image that resembles paper and an envelope. Letters appear in the stationery drawer as pieces of paper, not as postcards. There's also an urgent postcard if you want to make sure the message is read right away. The urgent postcard has *urgent* stamped on it, which will cause special handling when the addressee receives it. The urgent stamp is also available in the stamper, if you decide to make your message urgent after you've written it on a plain postcard. The *urgent* stamp on the postcard, letter, or envelope causes the special handling, whether it's automatically stamped or manually added.

If you use your communicator primarily for work, you might want to replace the plain postcard in the middle of your desk with the business letter. You can do this easily, and you can change it again whenever you need to. To change it, open the desk drawer where the stationery is kept and then slide a business letter out onto the desk. You can then option-slide the business letter onto the postcard in the middle of your desk, and the business letter replaces it as the standard kind of new message. Of course, you can always open the drawer and pick another kind of stationery.

Pay Attention. If you watch closely when you tap the new message image in the center of the desk, you'll see that the message springs out of the stationery drawer instead of zooming out of the new message image itself as you might expect. This is intentional. The idea is to draw your attention to the stationery drawer so that you'll go exploring there. By having the new message hop out of the drawer, Magic Cap's designers hope to lure you into learning about the different kinds of stationery.

If you don't find the kind of stationery you need, you can make your own custom stationery to keep in the desk drawer, the ultimate way to personalize your letters. When you create your own stationery, you can make original drawings or scribblings, or you can use the goodies that Magic Cap provides, such as stamps and animations. Start with a plain piece of paper by tapping *plain letter* in the stationery drawer; then close the name chooser, leaving the new message unaddressed and blank. Design your stationery to look however you want.

You might add a nice face from the stamper's *faces* drawer. If you're really hip, you might choose to stamp your stationery with the animated character that sits, sleeps, hops, and spins. After you've finished, you can slide the letter to the stationery drawer and it will snap into place. You can option-tap the keyboard image to open the keyboard with label maker, then type a name for your stationery and drop the label on it to give it a name. You'll have a new kind of paper that you can use when you want to send a letter with a personal and funny touch—and when was the last time you could send someone a letter that hops?

Out Box: Where Messages Go

Let's go over what happens when a message is sent, besides just the communication from you to someone else. Your communicator has an out box, which is a launching pad for messages on their way out. If there are messages waiting in your out box, you can open it to see them, or slide them out to stop them from being sent. Tap the out box to see the messages that are inside it. Figure 2-12 shows you what the inside of an out box might look like.

Although you can open the out box to see the messages inside, and even open the messages themselves, it's not a great place to peruse your mail. That's because mail in the out box might be getting sent while you're looking at it, and it's liable to get filed away while you're in there. If you really want to look at mail that's in the out box, you're probably better off sliding it out onto the desk, which will prevent it from being sent while you're looking at it.

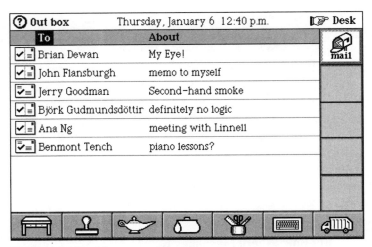

FIGURE 2-12. Messages in out box

You might think of the out box as a pretty simple place that just sends messages on their way, but Magic Cap and its Telescript components let you control your out box's behavior in a number of interesting ways. This control falls into two general areas: when messages in the out box are actually sent, and how they're handled after they're sent. These settings are controlled by rules in the out box.

When to Send Messages

Usually, you'd like messages that go to the out box to get the heck out of the communicator as soon as possible so they can get to their addressees. That's why the rule for when to empty the out box is set at the factory to send everything as soon as possible. If you're in the habit of making a bunch of messages at a time, you might want to change this rule so that you can write all your messages and then send them all at once.

If you're not plugged into a phone line and you don't have wireless hardware and mail access, this rule doesn't take effect until you're plugged in, and the out box holds all the messages until you're connected. Once you're plugged into a phone line, you can tap the out box to open it, then tap *mail* to send any messages that have been waiting around.

The out box also has a rule you can set that will empty the out box as soon as you send an urgent message. This one lets you keep the usual "send everything" rule turned off, but then sends everything when you fire off something urgent.

What Happens After Messages Are Sent

Whenever you send a message, the fact that you sent something is automatically logged with the time and date of sending, as well as a description of the message. The log is available by tapping *log* on the name card of the message's addressee. After you send the note, you could open the name card in the name file and then tap *log* to see when you sent the message and its description.

The out box includes several rules that determine what happens to mail after you send it. If you want to keep more than just a log, you can use rules to help file the messages themselves in folders in the file cabinet. There are three kinds of rules you can set for filing outgoing messages. You can file according to text in the message, you can file based on attributes set by stamps on the message (urgent, confidential, and so on), or you can set a catchall rule that will file everything not handled by the other rules. Figure 2-13 shows the three rules for out box filing that are set at the factory.

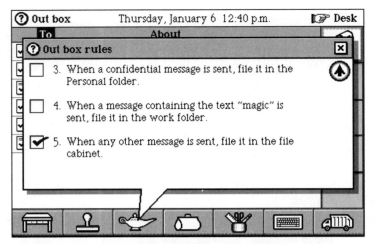

FIGURE 2-13.   Out box rules for filing sent mail

You might make a folder for health information and then set a rule to file everything containing the word "health" in that folder. You could have a folder just for urgent mail, which will provide you with a file to explain to your boss why you deserve a great performance review and raise. If only you could find a person this efficient to file the rest of the stuff in your life!

In Box: Where Messages Arrive

When you collect your mail from any services that you belong to, your messages arrive at the in box. To see your mail, you tap the in box to open it, then touch a message to read it. When you're looking at a message in the in box, you'll see the familiar arrows at the top of the screen that let you move to the next or previous message, assuming you have more than one message in your in box. There's a picture of this in Figure 2-14.

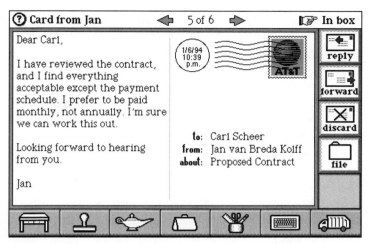

Dear Carl,

I have reviewed the contract, and I find everything acceptable except the payment schedule. I prefer to be paid monthly, not annually. I'm sure we can work this out.

Looking forward to hearing from you.

Jan

1/6/94
10:39
p.m.

AT&T

to: Carl Scheer
from: Jan van Breda Kolff
about: Proposed Contract

reply

forward

discard

file

FIGURE 2-14. Open message shows how many messages are in the in box

When you open the in box, you can collect your mail by tapping *mail* along the right side of the screen. When you tap *mail*, Magic Cap connects to the mail service and gets your mail.

When you're looking at messages in the in box index, the messages' images change depending on whether they've been read and whether they're postcards or letters. Messages that have been read have an empty gray rectangle, while messages you haven't opened yet have a filled-in white image. You can sort the messages in your in box by any of the headings (sender, date received, and subject) just by touching a heading.

You can file all the messages at once by tapping *file all*. You might want to file messages individually as you read them, but *file all* is a great option for people who like to set up specific rules for where mail gets filed, which you can do in the file cabinet itself. When you file with *file all*, all the messages go into the received mail drawer in the file cabinet, winding up in folders that you have set up to hold certain kinds of messages. See Chapter 8 for more information about setting up folders in the file cabinet.

If you're registered for PersonaLink, you can open the lamp and use the *summary* button to get a quick list of the mail waiting for you at the post office. You can choose which ones to have delivered to your in box, which to leave alone for a while, and which to throw away unopened. If you want to get rid of all your undelivered mail, the *clear* button does just that—it removes all the items addressed to you without bothering to get them.

In the real world, you don't have to bother with getting a summary of the mail that's waiting for you at the post office, and if you want to throw anything away, you can do so after it's delivered. Why do these commands exist? Delivering electronic mail costs you money and takes time, especially on a wireless network. This harsh reality requires commands like *summary* and *clear* that give you more control over which messages you receive.

Announcing Incoming Mail

Magic Cap's in box lets you exercise some power about how you want to handle incoming mail. There are two sets of rules that help you deal with your mail as it arrives. You use the first set to determine how Magic Cap informs you that you've got mail, and the second set lets you sort your incoming mail into folders in the file cabinet if you prefer to organize your mail before you read it.

You can set a rule to play a special sound for certain senders, with another rule playing a different sound when a message from just anybody arrives. You can set as many different "special sender sound" rules as you want. Another rule lets you instruct Magic Cap to display an announcement when you get a message with a certain attribute, such as *urgent*.

Sorting Incoming Mail

If you like, you can get your in box to sort your mail before you even open it. You can tell your in box to look for mail with certain special attributes, like urgent or confidential, and file those messages in a particular folder as soon as they arrive. Setting this rule tells Magic Cap to file your mail as soon as it's collected, before you even read it. This automatic sorting and filing feature can be very useful to people who get a lot of mail and need to prioritize how they read it.

You can set a rule that looks for some particular text and puts messages that contain that text into specific folders. This works for text in the message as well as certain senders. It's interesting to note that one of the places you can automatically "file" mail is the trash, which might be something you'll do if you get inundated with junk mail.

If you're a PersonaLink member, you can ask Magic Cap to collect your mail automatically at a set time each day. This lets you plug your communicator into a charger/phone line before you go to bed and tell your communicator to go to the post office for you and pick up your mail (of course, it really just calls up PersonaLink and gets the messages stored there for you, but saying it that way sounds more like real life and is more fun).

Going Downtown

In addition to telling your in box and out box how to behave, you can also go directly to the source and set rules for handling your mail before it gets to your communicator. You can go downtown to get to the AT&T

PersonaLink building (tap the upper-right corner to go to the hallway, and then tap it again to go downtown). Knock once on the building to open its doors and go inside. From the lobby of the building, you can perform several tasks, including checking or setting some mail-handling rules.

Telescript-based electronic mail services have a store-and-forward capability, which means that they hold onto your mail for you (that's the *store* part) and then send it along to you when you want it (that's *forward*). The mail service's building represents the place that does the storing and forwarding: It holds onto your mail until you're ready for it, at which point it sends mail to your in box, kind of like a post office would.

While you're in the PersonaLink building, you can set some preferences about how you want it to work for you. There are two sets of rules. One automatically forwards mail that meets certain criteria, and another automatically throws away certain mail. You can tap the mailbox rules sign to customize those settings. You can set a rule to forward copies of all messages from a designated sender to a designated recipient.

You can also arrange to forward messages about a certain topic to a specific recipient, such as forwarding a copy of all messages about baseball to Darin Adler. You can tell PersonaLink to discard certain messages before you've even collected them. If you're really sure that you don't ever want to read messages from a particular sender, or about a certain topic, you can set rules to toss them unopened. You'd better be really sure, though, because once they're discarded, they're gone. You can't even dig them out of the trash.

If you have a pager, you can set rules that tell PersonaLink to page you. For example, you might want to be paged for a message stamped *urgent* or any message from a particular sender.

Downtown of the Future

If Magic Cap succeeds, downtown will be a swinging place where you can use your communicator to connect to all kinds of information services and stores. You might imagine being able to visit a travel agent, request information on flights to Cleveland for a sales conference, and also find out about taking your family to Walt Disney World afterward. You might still prefer to talk to your brother the travel agent during his business hours, but if you suddenly need to make your reservations at 10:30 at night, you could use your communicator to take care of it. A clever Telescript-based news agency downtown could know about your interests, collecting and forwarding just the news that you asked it to find.

You can imagine that if you wanted to get more information about health care reform, foreign investment in Germany, and Pierce Brosnan, you could ask the news service to keep an eye out for those topics and send only articles that cover those topics. Then, depending on the rules you set for your in box, you could have these articles filed automatically into folders set up just for them, letting you read them at your convenience.

If you're one of the millions of people who loves shopping with catalogs or televised shopping channels, you'll definitely want to try going to an online store to browse or buy things. Zarko's Department Store could have pictures and descriptions of dozens of items for sale and include an easy way to use the communicator to send an order or dial a customer service operator. You might also specify what items you're looking for, such as gold earrings or flannel nightshirts, and then ask the store to let you know when those things go on sale or when new merchandise comes in.

Summary

Magic Cap was created for communication. Telescript, which is built into Magic Cap, offers smart messaging features that Magic Cap uses to make communicating easy. In addition, Telescript will be the foundation for information services, which will then be able to offer even more powerful communication features for Magic Cap users. One such service is AT&T PersonaLink, which takes full advantage of Magic Cap's features. PersonaLink also offers gateways to other conventional electronic services, such as CompuServe and Internet. If you subscribe to PersonaLink, you'll be able to contact anyone else on these and other services through the PersonaLink gateways. There will already be one or two messages waiting in the in box when your communicator first comes to life, and one will be a signup request for PersonaLink.

Making a new message is the central feature of Magic Cap. The postcard is the central item on the desk, and when you make a new message, it actually hops out of the desk drawer, showing you that there are other kinds of stationery for you to use. The stationery forms look very much like their counterparts in the real world. Postcards show the addressee on the right, and you can put your message on the left side (Magic Cap lets you extend the postcard's length as much as you need to). Letters can have business headings, and plain letters are just blank pieces of paper, but both have envelopes that handle the addresses and delivery choices.

Consistent with Magic Cap's strong integration of features, you can add an addressee to your name file while you're making a new message, and even add a delivery route (fax number, electronic address) while you're there. You can also send messages to multiple addressees and groups from the name file. It's easy to choose different delivery choices for each addressee, even for different members of a group.

Lists of delivery choices are constructed from the contact information listed on an addressee's card, as well as information from your name card about which services you subscribe to and whether those services have gateways to other systems. All fax numbers will be listed as delivery choices, because all Magic Cap communicators can send a fax. If you know someone has an account on a system that you subscribe to (or can reach via a gateway) and you don't know the address, you may be able to use a directory lookup feature of that particular service. You can address the message to just a single person, to multiple addresses, or to a group, and you can also send copies. Messages can be carbon copied and blind carbon copied, and you can even have replies forwarded to someone else.

Although the image that sits in the middle of the desk is a postcard, you can change it to anything else that's in the stationery drawer or that you make yourself just by sliding the desired paper out of the drawer and dropping it onto the image of the postcard while you hold down the option key. You can choose from a plain postcard, urgent postcard, plain letter, or business letter. The business letter automatically adds business-like headings to the top of your letter, but you can edit this by option-tapping the stationery to change the automatic typing. You can also stamp your company logo, or write in your company name and address as letterhead at the top of the business letter or the envelope. You can even design entirely new kinds of stationery to keep in the drawer for special occasions.

Your out box is customizable with rules that tell it when to send messages, as well as what happens to your copies of the sent mail. The in box also has rules you can customize. You can instruct it when to automatically collect your mail from information services, how to sort mail before or after it's read, and how to alert you to certain kinds of messages; for example, an urgent message should always tell you it's arrived—otherwise, urgent doesn't really mean anything.

PersonaLink acts as the post office, and it, too, has customizable rules for handling mail. You can ask it to sort your mail by certain senders or stamped attributes (urgent or confidential) or even to discard it before you've seen it. All of these different ways to handle mail may be a bit tedious when you're setting them up, but they let you tell your communicator when to "go" to the post office to collect the mail, to look for urgent messages and send them immediately, to watch for certain kinds of mail and file it directly into your junk mail folder, and to have the rest sorted by sender and delivered to your in box. The best part is that it all works just fine even if you don't change the factory settings.

You can take advantage of electronic information services that are available downtown. News retrieval services that can be customized to send you articles only about topics you have selected and retail and service outlets that offer you electronic shopping or airline reservations are just some of the possibilities available in a well-developed Magic Cap downtown, where everything revolves around the ease of communicating.

Chapter 3

General Features

What You See Is What You Get

I never heard this funny word *interface* until computers came into my life. Not only did personal computers change the way people work and spend their leisure time, the computer culture added many new words and new meanings of familiar words to the language. Well-known old words like *window*, *menu*, and *mouse* now need to be understood in context so that they're not confused with a glass opening, something to read at a restaurant, or a small furry rodent. The definition of *interface* in my slightly out-of-date dictionary reads, "a surface that lies between two parts of matter or space and forms their common boundary." Huh?

Nowadays, though, *interface* has spread beyond computers and is commonly used to refer to the part of a machine that connects with the person using it. Interface designers can be found everywhere there is a need to learn and understand how people use things, then integrate that knowledge into a product or process. Magic Cap was created using the premise of whole person thinking as discussed in the Preface, and every engineering decision along the way was made considering the effect it would have on the life of that whole person.

If you're reading this book from beginning to end, you may have wondered about the order of the chapters. The chapter before this one expects you to understand and use electronic mail even though it comes before this general explanation of Magic Cap features and concepts. There are two reasons the chapters are presented in this order. First, you shouldn't be bombarded with definitions and explanations before you've even tried to do something real with your communicator. It's much better to get some practical experience first before trying to understand the theory.

Second, you don't have to know all the definitions and explanations to do something with your communicator. If you've finished the *Getting Started* lessons, or if you've just played around with some of the items on the desk, you've learned enough about Magic Cap to know how to move around to different places and how to use the keyboard to send a message or make an appointment. The ability to figure things out easily is a hallmark of a well-designed interface. Now that you have actually done something practical, reading about some of Magic Cap's features in greater detail will be more meaningful to you.

Navigation, Scenes, and Windows

Magic Cap was designed to imitate how and where people work and communicate in the physical world. As mentioned earlier, Magic Cap creates its own world inside your communicator to represent familiar objects and places, and it lets you move from place to place to work with objects. This movement is called *navigation*.

Magic Cap begins by showing you items on a desk. By touching any item, you can use it, send it, open it, or work with it in some way. You can slide some items to move them to other places. You'll also see that some items hop when they're moving to different places, like a new message on its way to the out box. You can leave the desk and go down the hallway, seeing other rooms in the house. You gain access to those other rooms by opening the door with a touch. You can even leave home to find other buildings and storefronts outside on a street downtown.

Most of the screen (everything between the top bar and the bottom bar) is the current *scene*. The scene focuses your attention on the task you're doing right now by filling the screen. Some scenes correspond to places that you go in Magic Cap, such as the hallway or downtown. Other scenes are close-up views of items that let you work with them. For example, when you touch the clock to set it, the clock zooms up close and fills the screen; what you're seeing is the clock scene, as shown in Figure 3-1.

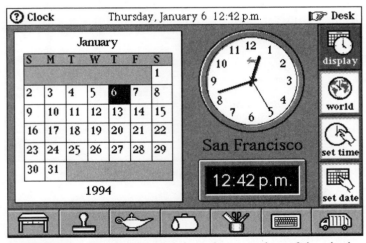

FIGURE 3-1. The clock scene is a close-up view of the clock

Some Magic Cap features must be made available without changing the scene. For example, when you're addressing a new message, you're looking at the message scene, but you also need to see the list of available names so you can choose your addressee. Magic Cap handles this situation by displaying a window that floats above the scene. Windows can perform additional actions or display information necessary to that scene. Figure 3-2 shows the name chooser, an important window that lists names.

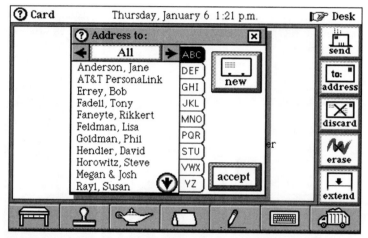

FIGURE 3-2. The name chooser window helps you address a message

The name chooser shows you all the names in the name file and even lets you add new ones when you're writing a new message. Another kind of window is for announcements, which tell you about events or situations that require attention. For example, when you get an urgent message, you'll see a window that announces the message, as in Figure 3-3. When you see an announcement window, you just read the announcement and then close the window.

FIGURE 3-3. Announcing the arrival of an urgent message

You'll also see windows with confirmation announcements. These windows are shown when you're about to do something irreversible, like removing a name card from the file. You'll receive a warning in a window with fancy borders and buttons that give you the opportunity to change your mind. For example, when you discard a name card, you'll see a confirmation window like the one shown in Figure 3-4. If you'd rather avoid these confirmation messages, you can turn them off; see Chapter 9 for details.

Do you want to throw away this whole card or page?

discard   keep

new

change

log

get info

discard

AB C

St

◆◆◆ hon
3 Yzern
Grosse
USA

◆◆◆ America Online ◆◆◆

RedWing

cellular
(313) 555-6521

FIGURE 3-4. Windows ask you to confirm destructive actions

Windowitis. Windows are a fine solution for organizing lots of information on a personal computer screen, but a communicator's screen is so small that piling up lots of windows would quickly create a confusing mess. Magic Cap's solution is using scenes, rather than windows, as the foundation for each related set of features. The alternative to scenes would be stacking up a window each time the user moved around, which would make a big mess. Windows are used sparingly in Magic Cap.

Most windows close automatically when they're no longer needed. Many windows have a button labeled *accept* that lets you signal that you're done with it. When you tap *accept*, the window closes. Windows also have an *x* with a box around it in the upper-right corner. Touching this box closes the window. Because Magic Cap tries to help you work faster, it often closes windows for you automatically, as when you switch scenes.

Magic Cap has another user interface goodie called a *choice box*. This one displays an option from a list and lets you pick what you want by touching arrows to move through the options one at a time. If you're impatient and you want to see all your choices at once, you can tap the label-like area in the middle that's surrounded by arrows, then touch the one you want. You already saw choice boxes in action when you selected different ways to send your messages in Chapter 2.

Smart Integration and Consistency

One of the main elements of Magic Cap is the tight integration of information across various scenes. If you find that you need to add a name to your list of contacts, you can do so without having to go to the name file scene. You can make new name cards while using the phone or the datebook, while making a new message, or from the name file itself. You can make a phone call while in any scene by using the *contact* button in the lamp, and then continue the call while you move on to other scenes. If you make an appointment for a meeting in the datebook, you can send a message inviting the participants without ever closing the datebook.

Magic Cap's designers worked hard to make features consistent and predictable. Things that look the same should behave the same, or users get confused and frustrated. Every time you learn about a feature, you will find that not only is its use consistent throughout Magic Cap, but you'll probably be able to guess about other elements of the feature by applying information you've already learned about other similar features.

Sound and Visual Effects

As soon as you start using your communicator, you'll notice that Magic Cap uses sound effects. These sounds help reinforce your actions as you take them, confirming that something has happened. Although most actions have accompanying visual effects, the sounds are a subtle reinforcement that you're getting what you expect. You hear a high-pitched sound when you make a new message and a pop when you touch the *x* to close a window. You hear the Magic sound at the beginning of the *Getting Started* lessons. When you discard something, there's a deep clunk. When you want to slide an object into the tote bag, you can be sure it's there when you hear the slurp sound.

As you use your communicator, you'll come to recognize the sounds that accompany familiar actions. Of course, you'll use your communicator in some settings that aren't appropriate for sounds, so you can easily turn down the volume. Because Magic Cap lets you customize your environment, you can also change the sound effects that are used for confirming actions.

In addition to sound effects, Magic Cap uses visual effects to confirm your actions. When you touch something, you can tell you hit the right spot because of the cross hair you see. Some objects highlight by displaying a kind of starburst effect that looks like cartoon motion lines. A simpler highlight effect, the one used by most buttons, is to invert the image—the background becomes lighter while the image becomes darker. While these highlighting effects sound strange when described, they're so intuitive that you'll probably understand their meaning right away without having to read about them first.

Magic Cap is filled with lots of other visual effects and animations that confirm your actions. In addition to mail that hops to the out box when it's sent, as already mentioned, discarded items often hop to the trash, filed mail hops into the file cabinet, and books hop onto shelves when you're done with them.

Top of the Screen

The very top and bottom of the screen contain things that you can always count on, no matter what scene you're in or what you're doing. The top provides various pieces of information about the scene and the communicator itself. The bottom has buttons that perform vital actions. This section presents a closer look at all the things that are available at the top and bottom of the screen.

The top-left corner of the screen always has the name of the current scene. There's usually a circled question mark next to the scene name that you can touch to get a description of that scene and instructions for the actions you can take there. The top-right corner of the screen always has a pointing hand and the name of a related scene. You can touch this hand or scene name to go there. Because tapping the hand or scene name often takes you back to the last scene you were in, this move is called *stepping back*.

As you become an expert navigator, you'll take advantage of a helpful shortcut built into the step-back hand. If you hold down the option key and touch the hand, you'll see a list of everywhere you've been (see Figure 3-5). You can get back to any scene instantly by touching its name in that list.

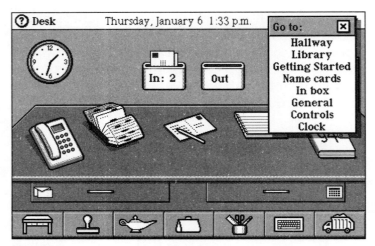

FIGURE 3-5. You can step back to any scene you've visited

In between the important areas at the left and right, the top center of the screen shows today's day and date, the current time, and the power level of your communicator's main battery. You can choose to display or hide any of these three items; details are in Chapter 9. If your communicator has some action that is ongoing, such as a message being sent or a phone call in progress, the top of the screen will also contain small images to remind you about those actions.

Bottom of the Screen

The bottom of the screen contains seven buttons that are also always visible, no matter where you are or what you're doing. Take a look at Figure 3-1, or virtually any other screen, to see the buttons at the bottom of the screen. The button in the bottom left corner has the image of a desk, and whether you're wandering around aimlessly exploring Magic Cap or you remember that you need to check your datebook while you're browsing in the library, you can always touch this desk button to return quickly to the familiarity of your desk. Because the desk button is always there and it always takes you to the desk, you know that whatever you're doing in Magic Cap, you're always just one touch away from a comfortable scene.

Next along the bottom of the screen is the stamper, a button with an image of a rubber stamp. The stamper holds drawers filled with stamps, animated cartoons, sounds, and even songs that you can put on messages and other pages (see Figure 3-6). Some stamps in the stamper also perform actions or assign attributes, like the phone number stamps in the name file, or the urgent stamp on a message. Each scene can add its own custom drawers, like the signature stamps that are seen only when creating a new message, or the label drawers in the name cards scene.

FIGURE 3-6. The stamper holds drawers of stamps

The lamp has buttons that help you communicate and do other important actions. Because the lamp is always there, you can perform these actions no matter what scene you're in (see Figure 3-7). The lamp includes *mail* and *fax* buttons to send the page you're seeing. You will also find the infrared *beam* button in the lamp, which you may remember from Chapter 2.

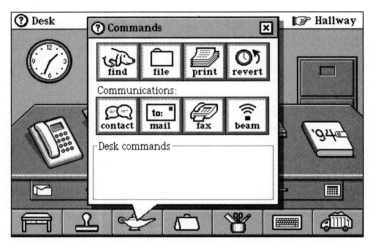

FIGURE 3-7. The lamp contains buttons that are always available

Another button in the lamp is *contact*, kind of a short-cut path to various means of communicating with someone. If you're in the middle of writing a letter to a client and you need to call your assistant to verify some information before you send it, you can touch *contact*, which then lets you use the phone or electronic mail, or you can quickly look up a name card without changing the scene. Like all other Magic Cap shortcuts, you don't need to know about or ever even use it; it's just another way to get there.

There are some other buttons in the lamp that perform general actions that aren't necessarily communication-related. The *find* button helps you track down information anywhere in Magic Cap. For example, after you've entered some appointments in the datebook (much more about that in the next chapter), you may want to go back and find one meeting in particular. If you don't remember the meeting's date, you can use *find* to search for it.

Touching *find* opens a window and the keyboard for you to type in what you're looking for. You can instruct it where to search and then unleash an animated basset hound (no, really!) to find it for you. The dog will search through the items on your desk until he sniffs it out in your datebook, opening to the correct date. When he's done, he hops back into the lamp until you call him again. If you just can't deal with an animated dog looking for your stuff, there's an option in the *Find* window that performs the search without showing the dog.

Sniffy the Wonder Dog. The dog that searches for your stuff is probably one of the most controversial aspects of Magic Cap. The designers of Magic Cap have a sense of humor but would never allow silliness to get in the way of the best possible experience for the user. People expect a dog to be able to search and find things, but not to be able to show human judgment; this expectation matches what happens when you search in Magic Cap, so the designers decided to use a dog. In practice, users either love or hate the dog, with very little gray area.

There is a *file* button in the lamp to move things into the file cabinet and onto memory cards; you can find out much more about filing in Chapter 8. The lamp also has a *print* button that lets you print information when your communicator is connected to a printer directly or through a personal computer.

The final button in the lamp is called *revert*, and it's there to make a last-ditch effort to retrieve something you thought was irretrievable. The *revert* button removes any changes you made to the scene before your current visit to it, saving you if you've done something you want to reverse.

In addition to these buttons that are always available, each scene can add its own buttons in the lamp that work only inside that scene. For example, when you're looking at a message, the lamp includes a button that measures how much the card "weighs" in bytes, giving you an idea about how long it will take to send. The lamp also includes rules that set policies for each scene. For example, the datebook has rules that tell how to remind you when an appointment is coming up and when the communicator should throw away old appointments.

Next to the lamp along the bottom of the screen is the image of a tote bag (Magic Cap's designers considered using a suitcase, a satchel, and even a pocket before settling on a tote bag). Think of the tote bag as the place where you can put something if you need to carry it from one scene to another. When you put something in the bag, you'll see the bag bulging a bit, a graphic reminder that there's something in there. When you take everything out of the bag, it shrinks back to normal size until the next time you need to carry something.

The next item along the bottom of the screen is the tool holder, which represents all the different tools you can use for writing and drawing. This is where you can choose from among different pens that you use for writing on the screen, when you make a new message. There are even some magical pens that draw all sorts of perfectly proportioned shapes, and others that draw lines that are always straight. Chapter 7 goes into greater detail about how to use the tools.

The next item is the button that opens Magic Cap's on-screen keyboard. You already know quite a bit about the keyboard if you followed the *Getting Started* lessons or if you've done any typing in any other scene. You've probably noticed some of the features that help you speed up your typing, such as smart capitalization and automatic completion of words. The keyboard lesson in *Getting Started* shows how to switch the keyboard from letters to numbers.

If you hold down the option key and touch this keyboard button, you'll get the extended keyboard, which lets you type letters, numbers, and special symbols like accented letters (Reneé) and international symbols (¡hola!). The extended keyboard also has a label maker that hangs off the top-right side. As you touch each key, the label prints out one letter at a time. When you're done, you can tear off the label and it becomes a text coupon that you can use to change an item's name. This is the process we used in Chapter 2 to name the custom stationery.

There are a few other keyboard goodies you haven't used yet, like the *expand* key. There will be more details about the *expand* key in Chapter 9, but briefly, you can use it to ask Magic Cap to guess the right word when you've only typed the first few letters. You can also set up abbreviations so you can touch a minimum number of keys while you're typing something, and then expand it to the full entry with the touch of one key.

The final button on the bottom of the screen shows the image of a garbage truck. As you might guess, this is where you throw things away when you don't want them any more. You can trash an item by sliding it into the truck; it makes a slurping sound when you drop it in there. As a precaution, the last few items you throw away are stored in the trash (its image changes to show that it has something inside) until you empty the trash by opening the truck and touching its *empty* button. If you're really desperate to recover something you've tossed, refer back to the explanation of *revert* for more details on whether it's really gone.

You can hold down the option key when you touch some of the buttons on the bottom of the screen to make them do other things. When you option-touch the keyboard, you get the extended keyboard and label maker. Option-touching the lamp lets you set the volume or go directly to the control panel. If you option-touch the stamper or tool holder, the window will open to the same setting it had when you last closed it. For example, if you have the *faces* drawer of stamps open and you choose a face stamp, and then decide you want another face, you can option-touch the stamper to go directly to that drawer.

In the Corner Pocket. The corners of the screen are precious real estate. Because you can figure out where they are without really looking, it's a good design idea to put very commonly used things there, and the desk button and the trash qualify. After you use Magic Cap for a while, you won't even think about the desk button— you'll just reach for the lower-left corner when you want to feel well grounded. Similarly, you'll get used to sliding things to the extreme lower right when you want to throw them away—and you won't even have to look to make sure they've reached the trash.

Construction

The engineers at General Magic had such a good time constructing the software that it seems they wanted you to be able to share in the fun. They realized that they couldn't possibly include everything that every user of a Magic Cap communicator might want to do, so they built a way for people to construct things on their own. The hallway includes a control panel that lets you put your communicator into *construction mode*. When you turn on construction mode, you'll get a magic hat that has an endless supply of goodies for building your own scenes: buttons, switches, choice boxes, sounds, borders, and lots more. If you just can't wait to find out about construction, check Chapter 10 for more details.

Summary

Magic Cap is designed to let you communicate easily with a minimum of instruction and background knowledge. The main scene is a desk, with several familiar items that help you communicate. You can go down a hallway to visit other rooms, like the library or the storeroom. You can go beyond the hallway and wind up downtown, where you'll find AT&T's building and other storefronts. As services become available, downtown will have more stores selling merchandise and services that will provide you with customized information.

The space between the top and the bottom of the screen is filled by the current scene. You'll see windows that provide more information, announcements, or confirmation buttons that let you double-check before you do something destructive.

The information you enter into your communicator is available in all applicable scenes. For example, you can enter a new name while you're using the phone, or send a message while you're working in the datebook. In addition, features behave predictably and consistently throughout Magic Cap. Magic Cap uses sound and visual effects as cues to help confirm your action when you touch the screen.

The top of the screen displays information needed for navigation, including the name of the scene, the name of a related scene that you can go to, and possibly the time and date and battery level.

The bottom of the screen has buttons that are available in every scene. The stamper contains drawers of stamps that can be used for decoration or to assign attributes necessary for sending or filing. The lamp holds commands that can be used anywhere in Magic Cap as well as rules that set policies in every scene. The tote bag is used to carry items from place to place, and it alternately bulges and shrinks, depending on what's inside. The tool holder contains various implements for writing and drawing.

The keyboard is used for typing, your main way of getting information into Magic Cap. The keyboard can type letters, numbers, and special symbols. The keyboard can also type text onto a label maker, producing coupons that let you give names to objects on the screen. You can throw things away by sliding them into the garbage truck, making the image change from an empty truck to a full one. You can retrieve recently tossed items from the trash until you empty it.

Magic Cap includes construction mode, a way for advanced users to put together their own buttons, switches, and other fancy features.

Chapter 4

Datebook

The Last Datebook You'll Need

Before I started using Magic Cap, I already knew how much I depended on my datebook to keep my life running smoothly. I noted business meetings, doctor appointments, work deadlines, carpool schedules, and the delivery schedule for bottled water. You probably have lots of other reasons for trusting your calendar. Because datebooks are such personal things, appointments are often written cryptically in personalized secret code, with start or stop times that don't necessarily match the lines they're written on, or directions to places that seem to be on other planets. Magic Cap makes it easy (yes, even fun) to enter appointments in a datebook so they'll be descriptive and complete, yet still personal.

The folks at General Magic built lots of shortcuts into Magic Cap's datebook to make entering appointments a snap. Like everything else in Magic Cap, the datebook and its appointments are easily customizable, and you can arrange and add items that fit your needs. When you enter a new appointment, lists of choices are offered for every part of an entry. There are several different kinds of appointment types with various descriptions and options. You can add notes, stamps, and alarms to any kind of appointment. Each kind of appointment also has its own identifying image, which you can change if you want to.

When you shop for an old-fashioned datebook in a stationery store, you can choose the style that best fits how you work—seeing a day, week, or month at a time. You might like to see a week at a time if you have enough entries to need more space than a monthly book contains. If you're really busy, you might have to put up with the bulk of a daily appointment book. Magic Cap lets you switch between all of those options with a touch.

In Magic Cap, you can enter new appointments while looking at a day, week, month, or even year. Switching between different views is easy, and appointments entered in one view show up in the others, of course. Figure 4-1 shows the datebook's day view. The first thing many people do when they get a new datebook is go through and enter important dates—birthdays, work events, anniversaries, vacations. Let's do that now with Magic Cap.

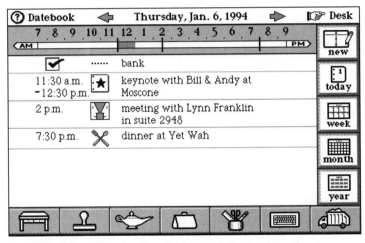

FIGURE 4-1. The datebook shows information about today's appointments

When you touch the datebook on the desk, Magic Cap automatically opens the datebook to today's page. When you touch *year*, Magic Cap displays the whole year, with today's date highlighted. The top of the screen shows the year, in case you've forgotten, and you can even wander off and look at other years if you want. When you touch a month, the month's view zooms open. As you might expect, the name of the month is also displayed at the top of the screen with arrows that move to the previous or following month. Figure 4-2 shows an example of a month view.

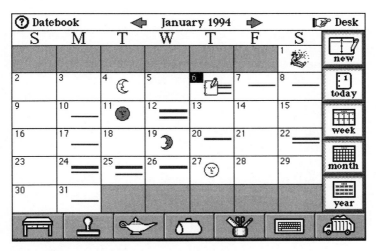

FIGURE 4-2. Month view in the datebook

Like most paper calendars, Magic Cap comes with some holidays already entered, both by name and by picture. You can change a holiday's picture or get rid of the occasion completely if you're a real curmudgeon. The datebook also includes appointments for turning daylight savings time on and off in the communicator's built-in clock. When the days arrive for starting or ending daylight savings, the clock is automatically adjusted, untouched by human hands.

Holidays and daylight savings time aren't the only special days the datebook knows. For example, the datebook offers a friendly reminder of what you need to do on April 15. Finally, you can set the datebook to have the month view show the phases of the moon if you're lunarly inclined.

Entering Appointments

When you tap *new,* Magic Cap offers several choices for appointment types. You can tap *birthday* (which is represented by a little piece of cake with a candle) to see the month and date, then pick the birthday person from the name file. If you don't have that person in the file yet, you can make a new name card right on the spot without having to go to the name file. When you tap *accept*, the new person is filled in as the birthday boy or girl, and there's a name card for the new person, who also becomes the current contact. If you want, you can attach notes to the birthday entry about how old the person is or what kind of presents you should buy. When you tap *save*, the birthday goes into the calendar. Because it's a birthday, the datebook automatically repeats that entry for each following year.

There's probably no better way to break in your new datebook than by adding your mother's birthday. Let's assume her birthday is December 24. After you've added Mom, you can enter your spouse's birthday; let's say it happens to be two days later, on December 26. Here's a cool shortcut for doing that: Hold down the option key and slide Mom's birthday entry to the tote bag. By holding down the option key while sliding, Magic Cap makes a copy of the birthday while leaving the original birthday in its place. Figure 4-3 demonstrates this.

FIGURE 4-3. Option-slide the birthday to the tote bag to copy it

Next, tap twice on the right arrow at the top of the screen to move to December 26, watching the Christmas tree go by as December 25 passes. The bulging tote bag is a reminder that a copy of the birthday is still inside. When you slide the birthday out of the tote bag, it pops into place. It still has Mom's name, though, so you can tap it to open, and then tap *who* and give the birthday your spouse's name. Not that you'd ever forget Mom's or your honey's birthday, of course.

The next appointment to enter is a favorite anniversary, such as your wedding. Start by tapping *year*, then tap to get to the right month and date. Tap *new* to make a new appointment, then tap *special day*. The special day appointment includes a *what* button; when you tap it, you'll see a list that includes *business trip*, *holiday*, and the one you're looking for: *anniversary*. (It also includes *hibernation*, an appointment that might be more appropriate for a bear's datebook.) After picking *anniversary*, just tap *save*, and the special day is set. You can see Magic Cap's list of special days in Figure 4-4.

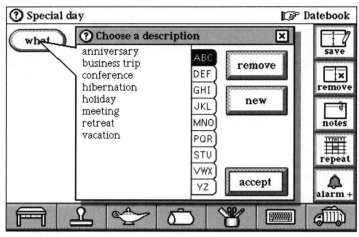

FIGURE 4-4.   List of special days

Making a List.   The datebook has several situations where you get to pick an item from a list, as when you set a special day appointment. In most of these lists, you can pick one of the built-in options, or you can add your own, usually by tapping the *new* button. When you add a new choice, Magic Cap is smart enough to remember the new option and will list it every time that list appears in the future.

If you want to add a new option quickly and bypass the list of items, you can tap the keyboard image at the bottom of the screen. The keyboard opens and you can type the new option immediately. Of course, the new option you create will be added to the list for future appointments. You can also remove options that you think you'll never use. If hibernation isn't in your plans, just tap it and *remove;* it won't bother you again.

Recurring Appointments

After adding all the birthdays and anniversaries to the datebook, you're ready to put in some of the other appointments that fill your time. You can start by adding the items that repeat, like staff meetings (twice a week) and school meetings (once a month). To make appointments that repeat, you start out by entering the first of the repeating events.

You'll enter appointments for staff meetings at the same time every Monday and Thursday. To put them in the datebook, you can just make one appointment for Monday and one for Thursday, setting each appointment to repeat every week. Go to the next Monday, tap *new*, and then tap *general purpose*, which is an appointment type that lets you pick the date, start and end times, what, where, and who. When you tap *what* and *where*, lists of choices appear; as usual, you can add your own. If you don't know (or don't care) about any of the information, such as location or end time, you can just leave it blank. (see Figure 4-5).

After you've filled in what you know, you're ready to set the appointment to repeat every week. To turn on the repeat feature, tap *repeat*. You can flip through the repeat choices until you see the right one: *repeat weekly*. When you save the appointment, it's entered for every Monday for the next year.

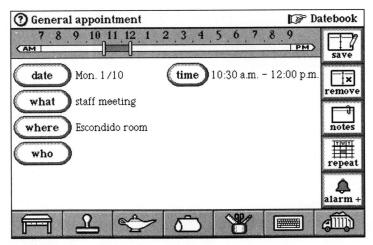

FIGURE 4-5. General appointment entry screen

Now you can set up the same appointment for every Thursday. You could just move to Thursday and enter the same appointment again, but let's try a shortcut. By holding down the option key, you can slide a copy of the appointment you just made into the tote bag. Then, move three days ahead, to Thursday. Slide the appointment copy out of the tote bag and just drop it on the day. That's it! Not only does it set up the new appointment, but Magic Cap is also smart enough to figure out that you want it to repeat every Thursday, since the original appointment was set to repeat every week.

School Daze

Now let's enter another repeating appointment, a school meeting. Once a month, on the third Wednesday, we'll enter a class meeting for the third grade class at Christa McAuliffe School. The meeting is always at 7 P.M. at school, and like many meetings, you never know when it will end. When you enter the appointment in the datebook, fill in 7:00 as the start time and just don't bother with an end time. The datebook's designers understood that lots of appointments and meetings don't have a scheduled ending time, so you don't have to pretend that there is one.

Because this meeting happens on the third Wednesday of every month, you'd hope to use the datebook's repeating appointments feature to add the meeting to each month's calendar automatically. By using the *repeat monthly by day* option, the datebook understands that this meeting is always on the third Wednesday and schedules it there for future months. It suggests repeating the meeting for a year in the future, which you can adjust to May instead. In addition to monthly appointments that repeat by day, the datebook also lets you set up appointments that fall on the same date every month.

In this way, you can enter the meeting for a single Wednesday night and easily have it repeated for the whole school year. The subsequent meetings are each individual appointments, so you can change them or remove them as necessary without affecting any others. This makes the datebook flexible enough to handle the inevitable postponed or canceled meeting without messing up all the others.

Engraved Invitations

Because I work freelance, timely scheduling of meetings has a direct impact on my income. If you're like most modern communication cowpokes, telephone tag drives you crazy when you're trying to get together with someone. To help with this problem, Magic Cap includes a slick system for setting up meetings that is centered around the datebook. We'll use this system to get a meeting going.

To set up the meeting, tap *new,* then *meeting* to get the appointment entry scene. As with other kinds of appointments, you can set the date and time. The *where* button produces a list of possible locations for the meeting. As always, you can choose one of those listed, or add your own. You could choose *my home* or *my office,* but it's always more fun to have meetings at restaurants—after all, that means you get to eat.

When you're ready to choose the participants in the meeting, Magic Cap shows off how it integrates all the information in the communicator. When you tap *who,* you'll see a window listing the people you can choose for the meeting (see Figure 4-6). This isn't just any list of people, though—it's the same names that appear in the name file. Magic Cap uses the name file as the center for any kind of communication, including meetings, messages, phone calls, and faxes.

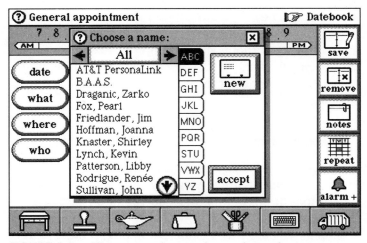

FIGURE 4-6. The name chooser is used to select names for an appointment

What if you need to make an appointment with someone who's not listed in the name file? The window that lists names includes a *new* button. You can tap that button to enter a new name card quickly, and you can then add that new name to the meeting. You even have access to the name file from the datebook, and you can add any name to the file for future lunch possibilities.

We'll set this up as a meeting at Seafood Sam's with three people, Martha, Steve, and Keith, and because this is a brand-new communicator, none of them is listed in the name file yet. By adding them now, you get to list them in the appointment, and you'll also have them in the name file for any future communication. To enter the new names, tap *new* and add the information for each person's name card in turn.

Choosing Names. The window that lets you pick from the name file is called the name chooser. It has a few other features that are especially useful as the list of names grows larger. There are tabs running down the right side of the list that let you jump quickly to any set of three letters—for example, if you tap the *STU* tab, the name chooser will make sure that the names starting with S (and T and U, if there's room) are on the screen.

The name chooser also includes a choice box that lets you see all the names, or only certain sets of names if you want. You can look at only the people, or just the companies, or you can choose to see only the members of a single group. One other note about the name chooser: The groups are shown in boldface so that you can spot them easily.

After you've entered the three names into the name file (without ever leaving the datebook and having to open the name file), you're ready to add the three new folks to the meeting. Magic Cap remembers that Keith was the last name card entered, so Keith becomes the current contact—Magic Cap will have Keith's name selected when the name chooser opens. If that's who you want, you can just tap *accept,* or you can choose another name, which will then become the current contact.

The current contact feature is handy here, because you do want Keith in the meeting. When you tap *accept,* the window closes and Keith is added to the meeting. This is OK, but now you have to tap *who* again to add Steve and Martha to the meeting. To make things a bit faster, Magic Cap defines this nice shortcut: If you hold down the option key while tapping *accept,* the chosen person is added to the meeting, but the list of names stays open. This little trick lets you pick all the meeting participants quickly. That's a perfect example of an option-key shortcut: If you know about it, you can work a little more quickly; if you don't, you can accomplish the same task with a more obvious (but longer) list of steps.

As the last step in setting up the meeting, you can use the priority and status features to set the meeting as tentative, but high priority. The tentative setting adds a question mark on the meeting's display in the day view and the high priority is designated by an exclamation point.

When you're done adding the three people to the meeting and putting in all the details, all three names appear next to *who* on the appointment entry screen, as shown in Figure 4-7. Of course, if you're having a typically busy day, you may find that you won't be next to a telephone for more than 10 minutes at a time, so trying to reach three people, confirm the details, and possibly change them would be tough. The people you need to talk to might be somewhere on the road during a long commute, or maybe staying at a hotel and having meetings of their own in several cities. It would be great if this new communicator could help you get in touch with everyone.

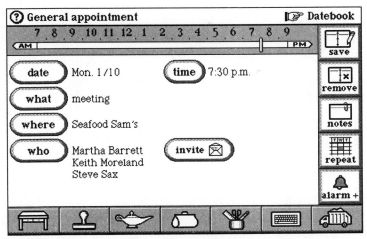

FIGURE 4-7. Meeting being entered with multiple participants

Here's how you can do it: Once you've chosen the meeting participants, a new button labeled *invite* appears on the appointment entry, with a suggestive little picture of an envelope. When you tap *invite*, Magic Cap automatically presents a new postcard that spells out the details of the meeting, addresses it to the people you want at the meeting, and asks for their response. The message uses the details of date, time, and place that you completed earlier, and even attaches any notes that you've entered along with the meeting information.

Not only does Magic Cap send a postcard separately to each invitee, but it also individually addresses each one, taking a good guess at the best way to contact each person (that is, via PersonaLink, fax, America Online, or whatever). Best of all, Magic Cap makes handy *yes* and *no* buttons for the meeting invitees to use when responding. Figure 4-8 shows the postcard that the datebook creates.

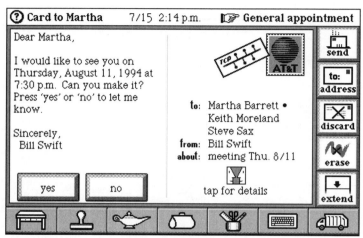

FIGURE 4-8. Automatically generated invitation for meeting

The postcard that Magic Cap creates is all written (very literately, I might add), addressed, and ready to go. If there's something about the message that you don't like, you can easily change it: You can write something with one of the writing tools, change the text by typing, or add a stamp or two. You can also change something more substantive, like the way that the card will be sent to any or all of the invitees.

You can mess around with the message for as long as you like. When you're finally happy with the message, you can send it. When you *send,* the message card hops into the out box, and a progress window shows what's going on as the message is sent. When the meeting invitees get their messages, there's a copy of the appointment attached for them to examine. Each invitee can simply tap the *yes* or *no* button on the message card to respond.

If an invitee answers *yes,* several intelligent things happen. First, Magic Cap automatically creates and sends a return message telling you that that person can come, adding a thumbs-up stamp to the return card (see Figure 4-9). Next, the attached appointment that you created pops into place in the invitee's Magic Cap datebook, substituting your name for the invitee's (that is, it doesn't give Martha an appointment that says "meeting with Martha").

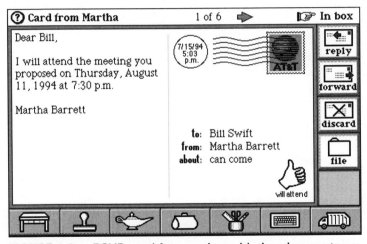

FIGURE 4-9. RSVP card for meeting with thumbs-up stamp

If all the invitees say that they're coming, the tentative setting for the meeting in the datebook changes to confirmed, and the tentative meeting's question mark is replaced with the regular face-to-face image that represents a confirmed meeting.

If an invitee taps *no,* Magic Cap throws away the invitee's copy of the appointment and then creates and sends a response telling you that that invitee can't come, stamping thumbs down on the response message. Of course, when you get the negative RSVP, the meeting stays tentative instead of being confirmed. If only one person responds yes, the meeting is confirmed, as Magic Cap errs on the side of caution, figuring that you'll want to go ahead with the meeting even if only one other person can make it.

This magical scenario of automatic response works great when both the sender and the recipient have Magic Cap, but what if one or more of the meeting invitees is using some other brand of communicator? If a message is received by a classic kind of mail, such as AppleLink or CompuServe, that doesn't know about buttons or datebooks, the automatic response and scheduling stuff obviously can't work—the invitee will have to send a response back manually. Magic Cap's electronic mail is smart enough to work wonderfully when communicating with advanced Telescript-based services like PersonaLink, and it works as well as possible when connecting to conventional services.

By using Magic Cap, you and the meeting's invitees don't need to rely on voice mail, answering machines, or hotel operators—the messages can be received and answered when it's convenient for the recipient. You don't even have to wait until the messages are sent before you can use other features, because Magic Cap lets you keep on working on other things while it's sending messages.

Also, the meeting invitees don't have to have Magic Cap to get the messages. As long as an invitee has one of the many electronic mail services that you can reach, or even just a fax machine, Magic Cap can get the word out. Now you can look forward to that dinner with your associates!

Integration

After all this inviting and responding, the appointment shows up in the datebook's day view as a *meeting with Martha and others* (it actually uses those human-sounding words) at Seafood Sam's at 7:30 P.M. This little exercise demonstrates one of the best features of Magic Cap—the amazingly tight integration of different kinds of information and communication. You opened the datebook and made an appointment, obviously something a datebook should be able to do. But while you were there, you added three people to the name file without having to actually open the name file. Then, you sent electronic mail messages to those people without having to go to the mail scene. This well-designed integration lets you get work done smoothly and quickly without having to fuss around with details of getting from one place to another.

To Do Lists

You probably don't have the luxury of being able to concentrate on just one thing at a time in your life—if you did, you wouldn't be interested in Magic Cap. Most people have a work life, a home life, a social life, and maybe a few other lives, and they need to remember different things for each one. Work life includes deadlines, schedules, and meetings; social life means sports, concerts, and parties; home life involves family, friends, personal finances, errands, and relaxation.

An old-fashioned appointment book is barely adequate for writing down where you have to be and when, and it usually has no place at all for keeping track of what you have to do. Many people like to make lists of what they're supposed to do and what they need to buy, and of course, they usually leave those lists at home when they need them most. Magic Cap provides help in remembering what needs to be done without having to buy cases of sticky notes.

Magic Cap's datebook lets you build and maintain lists of tasks that you have to do. When you're in the datebook, tap *new,* then *to do,* to enter information about a new task to be done. Let's make a task that's a reminder to go to the bank during today's lunch hour to deposit the checks that Junior got for his birthday from his grandparents. When you tap *what,* there's a list of descriptions for the task, and it's the same list that the datebook always shows when you have to fill in a description for any appointment. There's nothing in the descriptions about going to the bank, so you can type in a new description, *bank.* As *bank* is entered for the task, this new description is added to the list that will be offered whenever you enter a new appointment.

After you fill in the description, you get to choose the starting date and the deadline for the task. The new task suggests today as the start date, but you can tap *start* to see the date chooser and then use the arrows and the calendar page to move to a different date. The new task suggests one year from today for the deadline, but that's a little too long for this one; surely your mother-in-law would call long before the year was up, wondering why her check hadn't cleared. Again, by tapping *deadline,* it's easy enough to change the month, year, and date with the arrows at the bottom of the date chooser. Let's set the deadline for tomorrow. You can see the finished product in Figure 4-10.

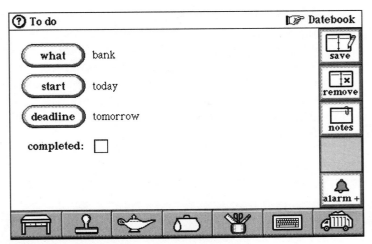

FIGURE 4-10. To do appointment entry

It might also be a good idea to add notes to remind yourself which account to put the checks in, plus reminders for other banking transactions you might want to make, like transferring money from the savings to the checking account to cover that check you wrote for car insurance. You can do this by tapping *notes* on the right to open the notes window. Then, write the notes, or tap the keyboard and type the notes if you're one of the many people who can't always read their own writing.

As you finish the notes and close the notes window, you can review the details of the task to make sure they're right. The task reveals another magical touch that's a welcome relief from the digital mindset of computers: The starting date for the task reads today, rather than giving today's date. (The datebook is also on a first-name basis with *tomorrow* and *yesterday*, but that's it—no *day after tomorrow* or *a month from next Tuesday*.) Like so much of Magic Cap, the datebook knows that most humans would use the word *today* when referring to an appointment that takes place on the current day.

You can make the same kind of entries for other errands and tasks, such as a trip to a customer's office to check on an order, a visit to the city government building to renew a business license, or a quick stop at the grocery store to get stuff for dinner. When a task is all filled in, you can tap *save* to put it into your datebook. The task is added to your list of appointments for the day, which you can see in Figure 4-11.

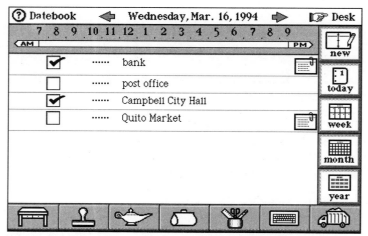

FIGURE 4-11. Day view of datebook with to do appointments

After you've completed a task, you can mark it off with the handy check box that appears next to the item in the datebook's day view. If you don't complete a task, it automatically reappears the next day, and the next, until the deadline comes. After the deadline passes, the task stops carrying forward. In the week and month view of the calendar, *to do* items are identified by a picture of paper and pencil at the top of the date, reminding you that there are things that need to be done that don't really qualify as appointments. The space below the date is reserved for real appointments.

💡 **Seeing into the Future.** If you're wondering why the suggested deadline for a task is a year away, here's the thinking of the datebook's designers. A *to do* item wouldn't be very helpful if you needed to keep adding it to your daily schedule until it was finished. The mission of a *to do* entry in Magic Cap is to move automatically from day to day, gently reminding you, as long as the task hasn't been completed and its check box is blank. When you reach the deadline and the task remains unchecked, it finally stops on that date. Since most people wouldn't have a simple task that takes a year to complete, the datebook can have 365 days to keep needling you about it, which should be plenty. You might imagine a future version of Magic Cap that warns you when an undone task is about to hit its deadline.

Day after Day

Magic Cap's datebook lets you schedule events that span multiple days. When you enter one of these, the appointment stretches out across all its days on the week and month views and appears at the top of each day's view during the event.

If you travel for business, you know that the best business trips are a mixed blessing, and the worst ones can be real nightmares. Let's say you have to travel to a customer's office on an extended trip, that is, one that will last more than just one day.

To enter the trip into the datebook, tap *new* and then *business trip* to get started. The entry screen for business trips is straightforward and very businesslike. You get to enter a description of the trip from a standard list of multi-day events, or (as always) you can add your own description, which will make it available again the next time you schedule a multi-day event. Then, you enter the date the trip starts and the date it ends. That's it. As with any appointment, you can add notes to remind you of any vital details. For this event, you can put your departing flight information in the notes.

The datebook knows about other kinds of appointments that span multiple days. When you tap *new*, you can choose from three different multi-day appointments: *business trip*, *vacation*, or *multi-day*, as shown at the bottom of the window in Figure 4-12. The first two, *business trip* and *vacation*, are really just multi-day appointments with the *what* information already filled in. If you choose the generic multi-day appointment, you can fill in the appointment description from choices that include *conference*, *holiday*, and *hibernation*, among others. Of course, you can add your own choices, too, and any new entries (as I'm sure you've already guessed) will be offered whenever you make a new multi-day appointment.

The day view has one image for *business trip*, one for *vacation*, and one for every other kind of multi-day appointment. The images are different only in the day view; week and month views simply show a line across the days of the event. All the multi-day appointments have space for a description, a starting date, and an ending date.

FIGURE 4-12. Three kinds of multi-day appointments

We've dealt with a business trip; now let's schedule a vacation. Let's imagine that your family is going to spend Thanksgiving at Disneyland. It's kind of a tradition for folks on the West Coast who find themselves far from their families for the turkey holiday. To get ready to enter this happy appointment, tap *year* to see the year view, then tap the calendar for November. You'll probably notice the image of the hapless, headless poultry on the fourth Thursday of the month—that's the week you're looking for (see Figure 4-13).

Now you can touch the day your vacation starts, and you'll see the view for that day. Tap *new,* and then *vacation.* The datebook suggests *today* as the starting date for your vacation—if only it were true. It's not, so you tap *from* to enter the starting date of your vacation, then tap *until* to enter the vacation's ending date. Both dates are entered with the same date chooser that you get used to seeing in Magic Cap every time you need to specify a date.

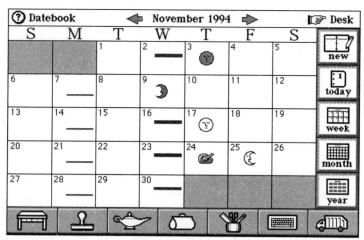

FIGURE 4-13. Month view for November

If you really enjoy your holiday trip to Disneyland, you might want the appointment to say *Disneyland* instead of *vacation*. Tap *what* to see the list of descriptions, then *new* to enter a new one. Magic Cap places a typing point in the right place and opens the on-screen keyboard, and you can type *Disneyland*. The new description appears with the appointment, and it'll be in the list the next time you make a multi-day appointment. Not only have you entered your Disneyland vacation, but the next time you make a multi-day appointment, Disneyland will be listed as a choice right beside the ones that are built into Magic Cap, as you can see in Figure 4-14.

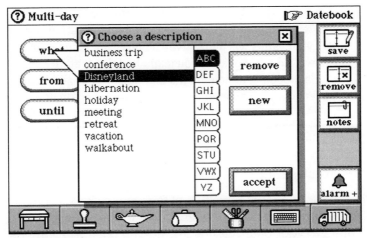

FIGURE 4-14. List of choices for multi-day appointments

Now you can add more detailed information about the trip by writing notes that include flight information and rental car confirmation numbers. You can get to the notes page by tapping *notes* and then typing or writing the notes on the screen. In a practically perfect future version of the datebook, you can imagine being able to attach a different note for each day, allowing you to enter specific information for each day and still enjoy the ease of a multi-day entry.

When you're done entering the vacation, you can tap *save* and see the appointment pop into the datebook. If you glance at the week view or month view, you'll see the vacation blocked out in November, right across that turkey image on Thanksgiving.

Busy Bodies. Do you ever schedule appointments that overlap? Lots of people do, some more than others. Magic Cap's datebook intentionally lets you make overlapping appointments, a process called double-booking. Making overlapping appointments is easy: Just do it. You can have as many appointments overlapping as your sanity will allow. Even if you're not in the practice of double-booking, you might find this feature handy for scheduling appointments during all day or multi-day events, such as a meeting during a business trip or a sky-diving session while you're on vacation.

Customizing

You probably have lots of favorite tricks for personalizing your paper datebooks. You'll find that Magic Cap caters to your creativity by letting you customize things to make it fit you better and more comfortably. You can do simple, helpful things, like changing the pictures that identify meetings, and you can also perform tricks that are a little fancier, like making a whole new kind of appointment.

Earlier in this chapter, you entered a repeating appointment for a monthly class meeting at school. The standard datebook image for a meeting, the face-to-face picture, doesn't really suggest a class meeting with the teacher and dozens of parents. You can fix this. While you're looking at the day view, you can tap the stamper and select the small picture of a blackboard. As you touch the blackboard, the window of stamps closes and you can slide the blackboard into place to replace the generic image for the meeting (see Figure 4-15).

You might remember that these meetings were entered as repeating appointments on the third Wednesday of each month. As you look at the class meetings through the forthcoming months, you'll see that they're now all represented by the blackboard image.

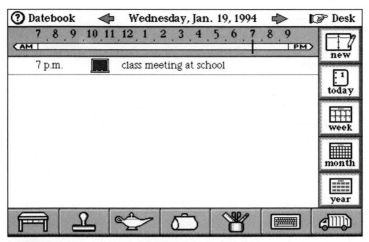

FIGURE 4-15. Customized image for a meeting

If you're a sports fan, you might spend a lot of time at the ballpark, stadium, or arena. When you go to a game, many of the details stay the same from one game to the next, just as with an appointment—*what* a game is; *where* the team's home is; and the *time,* which is probably the same for most games. (As fans of the San Francisco Giants, my family visits Candlestick Park for lots of afternoon games, but we avoid those frigid night games, so almost all our games start at 1:05 P.M.) The only things that change are the date of the game and the team they're playing. You can fill in *who* with the name of the opponent, if you don't mind having the names of hated teams in your name file.

To make it easier to schedule the games you attend each season, you can make a new general purpose appointment, fill in the *what*, *where*, and *time* parts of the appointment, and then tap *save*. When you see the new appointment in the day view, you can pick an appropriate stamp from the leisure drawer and slide it onto the appointment. Stamps for baseball, football, basketball, and other favorite pastimes are provided. The appointment is pictured in Figure 4-16.

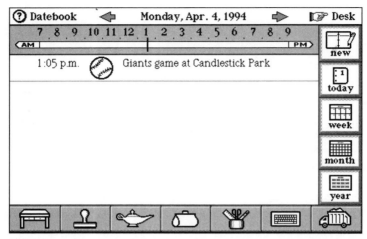

FIGURE 4-16. Day view with a baseball game appointment

Now for some magic: you can slide this appointment onto the *new* button, where it gets slurped up and added to the standard appointment types. From now on, whenever you tap *new*, you'll be able to schedule a day for going to see your favorite team play using a custom-made appointment type that has all the generic information filled in. Maybe a future version of Magic Cap will be able to tell you the score of each game before you attend.

Reminders

The datebook-makers at General Magic realized that appointments need to include a lot of special details. The datebook includes a button labeled *alarm+*, where you can set up some miscellaneous details about an appointment, including the appointment's status, priority, and alarm.

Because personal communicators are much better at remembering things than people are, you can tell the datebook to remind you of appointments as they come up. Using the *alarm+* feature, you can ask the datebook to remind you about an appointment from a week before the event to the scheduled appointment time.

If you know you have a deadline coming up on a project, you can ask the datebook to remind you a day before the deadline so that you have time to make sure that everything is ready. To do this, make a new appointment for the project, tap *alarm+*, and then use the arrows on the *alarm* choice box to see the options until you come to *1 day early*, the one you want to set. When you save the appointment and look at it in the day view, you'll see, as shown in Figure 4-17, that it now has a little bell as a reminder of its alarm.

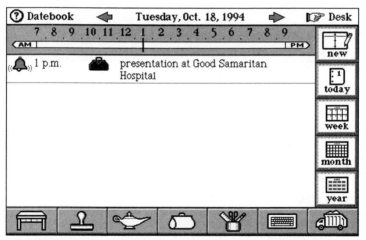

FIGURE 4-17. Day view with an appointment set with a reminder alarm

When you make a date to have lunch with a friend, you might worry about getting so wrapped up in working that you'll forget to look at the time, even though it's conveniently displayed at the top of your communicator's screen. When you set the lunch appointment, you can ask the datebook to remind you 30 minutes early so you won't be late—or at least you'll get to make an informed decision about being late.

Just exactly how will you be reminded about these appointments? As with many other features, Magic Cap supplies a standard way that this will happen, and it also lets you customize it if you want something different. For appointment alarms, the datebook will remind you in two ways: by playing the alarm sound (which sounds not unlike those irritating digital watches) and by displaying an announcement on the screen that will stay there until you close it. You can customize those reminders by changing the datebook's rules. See the "Customizing with Rules" section later in this chapter for more information about how to do that.

Appointment Priority and Status

Magic Cap can schedule appointments that might change or move around before they happen. Imagine that your father is planning a visit and you know the dates he's planning to come, but he might have to cancel due to a possible conflict. You can make a multi-day appointment in the datebook for the visit.

Because you're not sure if he'll be able to come, you'd like to make the appointment tentative. To do this, you tap *alarm+*, which gives you choices for alarm, status, and priority (see Figure 4-18). Use the *status* choice box to select *tentative*. When you save the appointment, it shows up in the day view with a wondering question mark to remind you of its precarious nature.

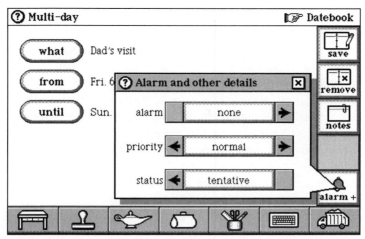

FIGURE 4-18. Multi-day appointment with alarm and other details window open

Let's assume that your dad lets you know that he'll definitely be able to make the visit. Now that you're sure he'll be here, you can open the appointment, tap *alarm+* again to see the appointment's details, and change the status to *confirmed*. When you tap *save* to close the appointment again, the mysterious question mark is gone, replaced by the more satisfying multi-day image that you've seen before.

Jump in Anywhere. A multi-day appointment appears on the day view of every day that it includes. If you want to change anything about the appointment, including its name, duration, or anything else, you can get to the appointment from any of its days.

Now that you're sure your father's coming, you can really look forward to his visit. In fact, you can use another datebook feature to reflect the excitement. If you open the appointment again and then tap *alarm+* one more time, you can use the appointment priority feature to tell Magic Cap that this appointment is very important by giving it high priority. When you save the appointment, the week and month views still show it listed as any other multi-day item, drawing a line from the start date through the end date, but in the day view the datebook reminds you that his visit has high priority by stamping the appointment with an exclamation point. He'd be really pleased with that.

Customizing with Rules

As mentioned earlier, the standard signals for appointments are the alarm sound and an announcement that stays open until you close it, but you can customize this behavior by using the datebook rules. You can choose to have both the sound and the announcement, or just one or the other. If you don't like the alarm sound, you can replace it with another sound that you're more fond of.

As you might recall, there are different rules for each scene, so make sure the datebook is open when you want to change its rules. After you open the datebook, tap the lamp, then *rules*. When you tap there, you'll see the first three rules that the datebook lets you set, as pictured in Figure 4-19. By tapping in the box or circle at the left, you can turn each rule on or off. The first two rules determine what will happen when an appointment alarm goes off.

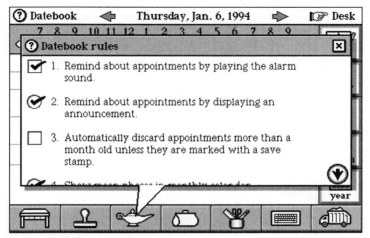

FIGURE 4-19. Datebook rules

The on-screen announcement is a great reminder for people who are easily startled, or for anyone who spends a lot of time in meetings or libraries. If you're more the aural type, you can use a sound to remind you instead of (or in addition to) the announcement. To turn the sound alarm off, just tap the check box at the start of *rule 1, Remind about appointments by playing the alarm sound.* When the check mark goes away, the rule is turned off, and you won't hear a sound to remind you about appointments.

Now, when an appointment alarm goes off, you'll get an announcement in a box on the screen. Even if the communicator is turned off, it'll come back on to display the reminder, and the announcement will stay there until you close it, which helps to make sure you don't miss it.

There are two kinds of rules in the datebook, those with circle check boxes and those with squares. The rules with circle check boxes are simply turned on or off; you can't customize them any further. The rules with square check boxes are flexible—you can play with them. The rule about playing a sound for an alarm can be customized by tapping the rule's text. Once you do that, you can pick any of the built-in sounds for the alarm, as you can see in Figure 4-20.

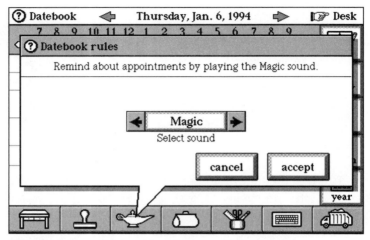

FIGURE 4-20. Customizing the sound played as an appointment reminder

When you've got the rule the way you want it, you can *save it*, making it the ruling sound, or you can *save a copy* of it and have a brand-new rule that uses this sound as the reminder, leaving the rule about the alarm sound just as it was. You could be really obnoxious and have both sounds (or even more), but that isn't a good idea for anyone who might be in a staff meeting when the alarm goes off.

Summary

The datebook is the place to tell Magic Cap about your appointments, and if necessary, have Magic Cap help you tell everyone else who needs to know. There are several built-in kinds of appointments to choose from. You can note birthdays that will automatically repeat every year, even though they're only entered once. Business trips can be scheduled across several days with a single entry, and personal notes are easily attached that stay with the appointment throughout its duration. Magic Cap can help schedule a meeting, and while you're entering that appointment, the touch of a button automatically creates and sends an invitation to the meeting's participants.

Your datebook becomes a gentle reminder of things you need to do, moving tasks from day to day until you complete them. You can even design your own type of appointment, reducing the amount of time spent entering the same event, like ball games or concerts.

There are various lists included in the datebook that cut down on typing because you can choose anything from the lists with just a touch. There are descriptions of the kind of appointments you can make, from serious (*staff meeting*) to light-hearted (*hot date*). There is a list of locations to choose from, ranging from *school* to *secret hiding place*. The datebook remembers everything you add, so the next time you want to schedule your acupuncture appointment, or enter the name of your favorite Chinese restaurant, it will be added to the lists of descriptions for you to choose from.

When choosing the participants of an event, the datebook displays the names in your name file, and even gives you the opportunity to add a new card for a new contact while entering that appointment. An appointment can tag along on an invitation to a meeting, and if the invitee responds positively, it will deposit itself in the invitee's Magic Cap datebook.

You can customize each event with notes. You can give an appointment instructions to repeat itself at certain intervals, and you can ask your datebook to remind you about the appointment with a sound or announcement.

Like the rest of Magic Cap, the datebook is designed to reflect the way you live and work. While you're at work, you might need to remind yourself to stop at the video store on the way home to pick up one of the movies little Zuzu wants to see. When you're at home, you'll need a place to write down the date of the big communication meeting at work, as well as some ideas about what to include in your presentation. The datebook works with the rest of Magic Cap to help you run your life.

Chapter 5

Name Cards

Keeping In Touch with Everyone

I'm usually pretty good at remembering the birthdays of family members and friends, especially when they happen to be on otherwise memorable days, like December 7 or April 1. I'm also good at remembering to buy birthday cards for friends early enough to mail them to arrive on time. If I were really together, I'd also remember to jot down my friends' addresses before I went to the card store so that I could buy them and mail them all in one trip. But by the time I get home, write out the card, get the address, and mail it, I usually need a belated birthday card. I've never been able to get in the habit of carrying an address book around with me all the time. Magic Cap's name file lets you have all the addresses you need (even if it's only once a year) right there with you all the time, neatly tucked inside a communicator that you'll be carrying around with you anyway.

The name file gives you a place to list lots of names, addresses, and telephone numbers that you can look up whenever you need to use them. Magic Cap itself also uses the name file to hold the details of how to make electronic contact with people, companies, and services. When you address an electronic mail message or a fax to someone with your communicator, you choose the recipient from the name file.

Even without considering electronic mail, the name file is a versatile address book. It has room for the names and addresses of all the important people in your life, and it is powerful enough to replace your paper address books (it seems that many people have more than one). The name file doesn't have cute pictures of cats on it like a paper address book might, but Magic Cap's personalizing features probably make up for that.

The name file can have cards for people you work with, people your spouse works with who you might need to be in touch with, companies that you do business with, or information service providers that send you stuff via electronic mail. The name file is flexible enough to hold many addresses, telephone numbers, and electronic mail addresses on every card.

Communicating

Remember that the information in the name file isn't just for you; your communicator uses the name cards to know how to reach your contacts electronically. You can use your communicator to get in touch with just about anyone in the name file, whether that person has a Magic Cap communicator, a traditional electronic mail address, a fax machine, or just a telephone.

The name file can automatically dial telephone numbers for you. All you have to do is find the card for an associate, hold the communicator next to the telephone's mouthpiece, and then tap a telephone number on the name card. Magic Cap will dial the number for you (this trick doesn't work with all Magic Cap communicators and all telephones). Your child can borrow your communicator to write a thank-you note to his grandmother for a birthday present; because you convinced her to buy a communicator, the note gets delivered quickly with electronic mail.

Entering Name Cards

One of the first things you'll want to do with a new communicator is fill up the name file with the names of your co-workers, associates, and friends. After all, it's not a very personal communicator without them. Let's start by adding a name card for our co-worker Susan Anthony. To start entering her new card, tap the name file on the desk. The name file zooms open and shows you the card for the last contact you made. When you tap *new*, you'll get to choose whether to make a new card for a person, company, group, or information service (Figure 5-1).

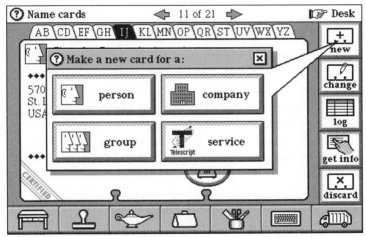

FIGURE 5-1. Window offers choices to make a new card

When you choose *person*, a blank card for the new person is made; a window to enter the first and last names appears; and the on-screen keyboard automatically opens, ready for you to start typing a first name. As you type the first two letters, *S u*, Magic Cap guesses that you're typing *Susan* and automatically completes the word for you. Tap *last name*, then type *Anthony*, then *done* to finish entering the name.

Sweating the Details.   Because entering names is one of the most common and tedious tasks you'll have to do with your communicator, Magic Cap's designers spent a lot of time making it as fast and convenient as possible. When you're entering a name card, lots of things happen to make your life easier. Some of them are so subtle that you may not even notice.

First, when you begin to enter the name, the box for *First name* already has a typing point in it, and the on-screen keyboard is already open, sparing you from having to worry about those two details. Next, you might notice that the keyboard is already shifted to uppercase for starting the name, the way most people like it. It'll switch back to lower case after typing the first letter.

Typing with the on-screen keyboard has been designed to feel comfortable and fast. The keys feel very responsive, working right away when you touch them and sounding a satisfying snap that suggests an electric typewriter.

Another touch for making typing convenient is automatic completion of words. As you might remember from Chapter 3, Magic Cap keeps lists of common words in various categories, such as first names, last names, cities, ZIP codes, and more. As you enter information, Magic Cap checks to see if your entry looks like one it already knows about. For example, as you enter the first two letters of *Susan*, Magic Cap sees that its list of first names contains only one entry that starts with *S u*, so it guesses *Susan* for the whole name but keeps the rest of the letters selected. If you're really typing *Sunshine* or you don't even notice that it's guessed and you keep typing the rest of *Susan*, Magic Cap's guessing won't get in your way as you continue typing. The letters you type will simply replace the letters it guessed.

As you enter new words, they're automatically added to the list of words that Magic Cap will guess when you're typing. You can get finer control over the words by looking at the Word Lists book in the library. See Chapter 9 for more information on using the Word Lists book to customize your words.

In addition to automatically completing words, Magic Cap knows about a couple of other things that can speed up your entries. If you're entering someone's work address and Magic Cap already knows the address for the person's company, it will guess that address so you don't have to type it. If you enter a city that it's already seen, it will try to guess the ZIP code. If you enter a two-letter state abbreviation but forget to capitalize the second letter, it will remember for you. It tries very, very hard.

After you tap *done*, the new card appears with places to add work and home addresses, work phone, work fax, and home phone (see Figure 5-2). You can add even more stuff by opening the stamper and getting stamps for other addresses and phone numbers—the name file will even accommodate your gadget-happy friend who has ten different phones. We'll look into that a little later.

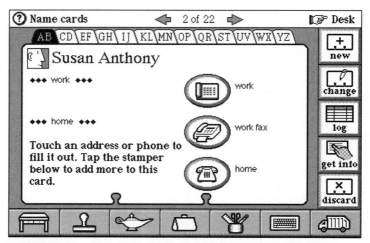

AB CD EF GH IJ KL MN OP QR ST UV WX YZ

Susan Anthony

♦♦♦ work ♦♦♦

work

♦♦♦ home ♦♦♦

work fax

Touch an address or phone to
fill it out. Tap the stamper
below to add more to this
card.

home

new

change

log

get info

discard

FIGURE 5-2. New name card awaiting more information

It Can Be Taught

In its efforts to help you enter information as quickly
and easily as possible, Magic Cap picks up a few tricks
as it goes along. Let's say we're now ready to enter Susan Anthony's husband, Mark. Tap *new*, then *person*,
then start entering his name: first *M a r k*, then the last
name. A *n* is as far as you get when Magic Cap guesses
that the last name is going to be Anthony and fills in the
rest for you. Of course, it learned the name Anthony from
your previous entry and suggested it here to try to save
typing. In this case, it guessed right, so you can just tap
the *done* button and Mark Anthony is entered.

What if Magic Cap guesses wrong and suggests a word
that's not what you want? You can find out by entering
another person, Hans Anderson, to the name file. Tap
new, and then *person* to start entering the new name

card. Typing *H a n s* is uneventful; this seems to be the first time Magic Cap has heard of that uncommon name. But when you type *A n* to start the last name, Magic Cap guesses Anthony, as usual (see Figure 5-3).

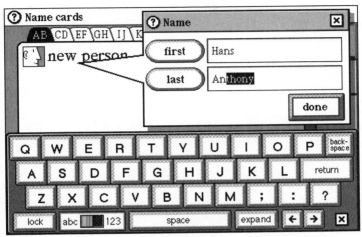

FIGURE 5-3. Magic Cap guesses for automatic completion

What do you have to do to correct this wrong guess? Nothing at all. As you type the next letter, the *d* appears and the rest of the wrong guess vanishes. You continue typing the rest of the name: *e r s o n*, then tap *done*. Magic Cap makes the new name card and learns a new last name, Anderson.

The next time you enter a last name that starts with *An*, Magic Cap won't make a guess at all. Instead, it will wait for the third letter of the last name. If you type a *t*, it will guess Anthony, and if you enter a *d*, it will guess Anderson. If you enter another letter entirely, it won't guess at all, but it will learn a new name for future guesses.

To make better guesses, Magic Cap keeps track of words in several different categories and only guesses them where appropriate. For example, it will never guess a last name when a job title is requested. Magic Cap comes from the factory with lists of common words in such categories as cities, job titles, and names (first and last). As you enter more name cards, the lists build. You can see and change the lists by looking at the Word Lists book in the library; there's more about that in Chapter 9.

Adding Addresses and Telephone Numbers

When you enter a new person, Magic Cap provides spaces for home and work addresses and home, work, and work fax telephones. Now you can fill in some of those addresses and phone numbers on Hans Anderson's name card.

Tap *work address;* the keyboard appears automatically, as usual, and you can type in a job title, company name, address, city, state, and ZIP. As you type each item, Magic Cap is working to make it easier for you by shifting the keyboard to uppercase when it thinks that's the right thing to do, guessing the rest of words you're typing, and doing other tricks to try to reduce the amount of typing you have to do.

To enter a phone number, tap *work phone.* As the keyboard and the entry window appear, Magic Cap has already suggested an area code. If it's the wrong one, you can just replace it. When you enter phone numbers, you don't have to bother with niceties such as parentheses around the area code or a hyphen after the first three digits of the number; Magic Cap will format the number for you. You can even use the mnemonic letters that appear on a phone dial next to the numbers, so when you enter 555-RIBS, the phone number of your favorite source of charred mammal flesh, Magic Cap will understand that you mean 555-7427. Figure 5-4 shows Hans Anderson's card with his address and phone number entered.

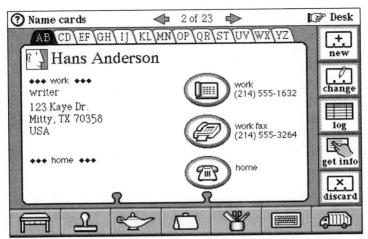

AB CD EF GH IJ KL MN OP QR ST UV WX YZ

Hans Anderson

♦♦♦ work ♦♦♦
writer
123 Kaye Dr.
Mitty, TX 70358
USA

♦♦♦ home ♦♦♦

work
(214) 555-1632

work fax
(214) 555-3264

home

new

change

log

get info

discard

FIGURE 5-4. New name card with phone and address information

I Got You, Babe. In working to make Magic Cap as useful and magical as possible, Magic Cap's designers tried to think of everything that people would do with their communicators. One interesting problem arose when entering name cards for people with only one name, like Madonna (and certainly she would be in lots of name files). Because these folks had no last name, they were filed incorrectly. The Magic Cap team noticed the problem and fixed it, and now single-name people are filed correctly—Madonna shows up after Chris MacAskill and before Julie Madsen, right where she belongs. The Magic Cap team referred to this problem as the Cher bug.

If you fill in all the addresses and phone numbers provided and you need some more, you can add them easily at any time. To add them, tap the stamper that's always on the bottom of the screen and you'll see lots of different kinds of phones and addresses to choose from, including fax number, pager, cellular phone, and work address (see Figure 5-5). If you want to add an address or phone that you don't see, you can use the *other* items and type in your own description.

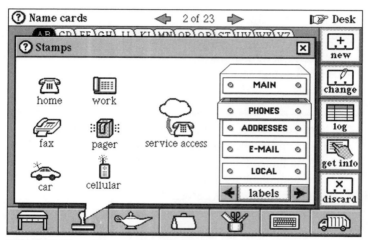

FIGURE 5-5. Phones drawer in the stamper shows additional choices

Each time you add an item from the stamp drawer, the image hops onto the card and zooms open for your typing. Let's say you want to add a cellular phone number for Hans Anderson. Tap the stamper, the *phones* drawer, and then the *cellular* stamp. The little phone leaps onto the name card, the keyboard appears, and a window opens with a place for you to type the phone number. When you tap *done*, the window closes and the phone number has been added to Hans's card.

You can continue to add new people to your name file. The more names you enter, the smarter Magic Cap gets about guessing words. This works especially well when you're adding members of your family (you'll really love it if you have a long last name and lots of brothers and sisters).

Name Card Commands

Like many Magic Cap scenes, the right side of the screen is filled with buttons that activate various commands. We've already worked through the first (and most important) command, *new*. The rest are *change*, *log*, *get info*, and *discard*.

After you enter a name card's initial information, you know that it's only a matter of time before something changes, whether it's a new phone number or address, or a whole new last name for a friend who just got married. To avoid changing something inadvertently, you have to tap *change* before typing in a change to any information on a card that's already been completed. While you're changing information, the items on the name card are drawn with boxes around them (see Figure 5-6). When you're done changing a card, tap *change* to lock it up again. If you're just adding information, such as an additional phone number, you don't have to tap *change* first. While you're changing, you can also throw away any information on the name card.

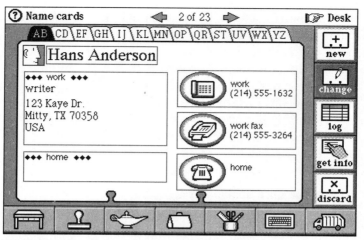

AB CD EF GH IJ KL MN OP QR ST UV WX YZ

Hans Anderson

♦♦♦ work ♦♦♦
writer
123 Kaye Dr.
Mitty, TX 70358
USA

♦♦♦ home ♦♦♦

work
(214) 555-1632

work fax
(214) 555-3264

home

new
change
log
get info
discard

FIGURE 5-6. Making changes to a name card

🪔 **Change for the Better.** You can also use *change* as a
shortcut to save yourself some typing. You might want to
have separate name cards for members of a couple
(we'll call them Louis and Jennifer). Even though they
have the same home phone number and address, they
have separate birthdays. Start by making a name card
for Louis, including home address and phone number.
Tap *change*, slide the address to the tote bag, and then
hold down the option key while sliding a copy back out of
the tote bag and dropping it on Louis's card. The option
key makes sure that there's still a copy of the address in
the bag.

Next, move to Jennifer's card and slide the address
out of the tote bag and onto her card. You can repeat this
process for their phone number. This trick lets you type
their home and work information only once, and then
copy it to use on separate name cards.

The *log* button lets you see a record of communication with someone. When you tap *log*, you'll see a list of the times you contacted the person or company on that name card. The *get info* button asks PersonaLink to try to find a name in its directory. If PersonaLink succeeds in finding the person, you'll get a certified name card for your name file.

The last button on the right is *discard*, which lets you get rid of the name card you're looking at. After you confirm that that's what you really want to do, Magic Cap folds up the card and tosses it into the trash.

Looking at Name Cards

While browsing through the name file, you can see several different views of name cards, all designed to look like they came from printed address books. The name file highlights the alphabetical tab with the appropriate letter pair at the top of the screen (for Hans Anderson, that's *A B*). You can also see how many cards are in the file and which card is showing, as well as left and right arrows to move forward and backward through the file.

If you want to see the names you have for any two-letter tab, you can tap right on the tab to go to that index card. When you do, you'll see a lined index card with a list of names beginning with *A* and *B,* as in Figure 5-7. There's also a power user shortcut: If you hold down the option key while tapping on a tab, you skip past the index card for that tab and go straight to the first card of the second letter listed. If there are no entries for the second letter of the pair, you'll just see the index card. So, if you option-tap on the *A B* tab, you'll see the first name card that falls under *B*, if there is one.

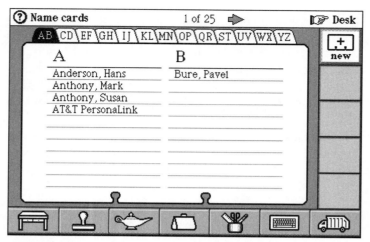

AB CD EF GH IJ KL MN OP QR ST UV WX YZ

new

A

Anderson, Hans
Anthony, Mark
Anthony, Susan
AT&T PersonaLink

B

Bure, Pavel

FIGURE 5-7.   Index view of name cards

When you're looking at an index card, you can open any individual card by tapping it. When you do that, the card you chose will appear. When you're looking at a name card, you'll also notice that the appropriate tab is highlighted at the top of the screen. In fact, when you tap *new* to make a new card, the name file highlights the *O P* tab (for *new person*, of course) as the card appears. This works when entering a card for a company, too, putting the company card under *M N* (*new company*) until you type in the company's name.

Because you need to alphabetize both people and companies in the same file, the name file's alphabetizing rules work equally well for companies and people (even people who only have one name, like Cher and Dad).

🪔 **Forgiving Users.**   As Magic Cap was being developed, potential users were brought in and asked to try out features while video cameras rolled. The development team then watched the tapes to see how well the user interface worked. This experience proved amazingly revealing and often painful, as the developers' clever designs sometimes delighted, but sometimes missed the mark completely, causing the designers to start over and try again.

One interesting problem appeared when users were typing in the first and last name for a new person's name card. Often, users would type the first and last name on the same line in the entry window, separated by a space, even though that line clearly says *first name*. This created a horrible situation. Instead of a person whose first name is Sergei and last name is Makarov, you'd get someone with no last name at all, which would cause the card to be misfiled and mess up any addressing to that person. How could users be taught not to do this?

Somebody had a better idea. Instead of requiring users to be taught something, they taught Magic Cap to see if two names were entered in the *first name* box and none in the *last name* box. If so, Magic Cap assumes that the user just typed the whole name at once and takes what the user typed and divides it into first and last names. This feature is so subtle that most users who run into it will probably not even notice that it's happened, but they'd surely notice if it didn't work right.

Current Contact

Magic Cap remembers the name from the last name card you see and keeps track of it as the *current contact*. Right now, the current contact is our old friend Hans Anderson, because we're still looking at his card. When you close the name file to go to another scene, Magic Cap remembers the card you were looking at. The next time you want to send a message or a fax, or make a telephone call, Magic Cap guesses that you may well want the current contact to get the message, as Figure 5-8 shows when a new message is created.

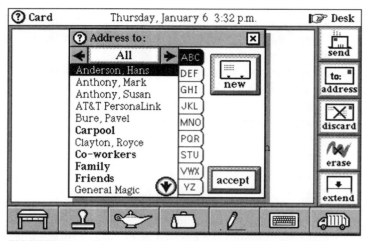

FIGURE 5-8. Current contact shown in new message name chooser

If you don't want to use the current contact, you can pick any name from the name chooser, of course, but Magic Cap guesses that since you just added the name to your file, or just got done looking at it, you might want to get in touch with that person. If you choose another name, the current contact changes to show your new preference. If you go to the datebook to schedule an appointment, the current contact is highlighted in your choices of *who*. The next time you open the name file, you'll see the last card you were looking at when you had the name file open, and that card then becomes the current contact.

Here's an example of how this current contact stuff can work even if you're not sending any messages. Let's say you get a phone call from Megan Marlowe, inviting you to a meeting tomorrow to discuss a possible work project. You tap the datebook to schedule the meeting. Because you haven't entered Megan in your name file yet, you can do that without having to close the datebook, as shown in Figure 5-9. While looking at the name chooser in the datebook, you can tap *new* (the button even looks like a name card) to add her name to your file. Later, after you're off the phone and you look in the name file, it opens to her card so you can add her address and telephone information.

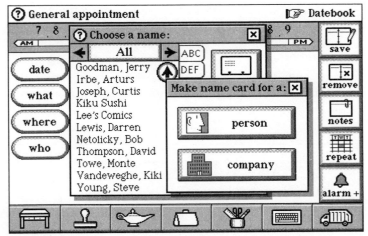

FIGURE 5-9. Adding new name cards from within the datebook

How You Get Name Cards

One way to add cards to your name file is to enter them directly, but that isn't the only way. As you've seen, you can enter new names while you're doing other things without having to stop and open the name file. For example, when you're in the datebook, you can schedule an appointment and create the name card while making the appointment. The next time you open the name file, you'll find a name card for the person or company you just added.

Whenever you get a message from PersonaLink, you'll get a name card for the message's sender. If you already have a card for the sender, Magic Cap makes sure that you've got the latest information about the sender. This helps keep your name file up to date as you keep in touch with people who send messages to you. After all, this is a communicator, not a notepad.

When you start using Magic Cap, one of the first things you do is enter your own name card to personalize your communicator. After you type your name, Magic Cap adds a *certified* sash across the bottom-left corner (see Figure 5-10), which means the card has "official" information, that is, it's either about the person using the communicator (that's you) or it was obtained from some official source (usually PersonaLink).

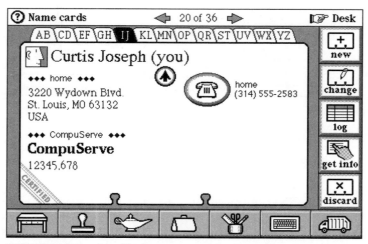

FIGURE 5-10. Certified name card for the owner of the communicator (you)

After you've typed in your name, you can go back any time and add other information, like addresses for home and work, all your phone numbers, and any electronic mail addresses you might have acquired. Then, whenever you send a message, your name card tags along and updates the recipient's name file with your latest information. Magic Cap knows that you've got the latest information about yourself, so it will replace outdated stuff in someone else's file with anything new and improved from you.

You can also add name cards for companies. In fact, you'll find a few company name cards already in your brand-new name file, giving you a way to get in touch with some of the companies that worked on making your communicator. Go ahead—give them a piece of your mind.

You can also add cards that represent Telescript-based services. These services will be few at first, but if General Magic succeeds in making its software platforms popular, many more services will spring up. You'll be able to join these services to get new kinds of information from distant places. Usually, you'll get a name card for every service that you join, but you may be able to get information from some services by manually entering a name card and then sending a message. Watch your in box (and the skies over downtown Magic Cap) for information on future services.

Electronic Mail Addresses

Earlier you saw that the stamper is filled with lots of choices for addresses and phone numbers, but you should look in the *E-mail* drawer to find the real magic of a personal communicator. In that drawer, pictured in Figure 5-11, you'll find logos for lots of traditional electronic mail services, such as America Online, Prodigy, and MCI Mail. As you enter new name cards, you can add addresses for these traditional services, because not all your contacts will be available on Telescript-based services.

FIGURE 5-11. E-mail drawer in the stamper shows some information services

You can use these stamps to send messages to your contacts who have addresses on many different kinds of electronic mail. There are two ways to reach people using different services. First, your communicator has software packages that let you talk directly to some electronic mail services, including PersonaLink. Second, you can use these services to forward mail to other services by using *gateways*, special connections from one mail service to another.

Using gateways, you can get from PersonaLink to almost any other electronic mail service. For example, if an associate of yours has a CompuServe address, you could enter that address on your associate's name card. Then, you could create a new message addressed to your associate. One of your delivery choices for the message would be *CompuServe via PersonaLink*, which means that your message would go to PersonaLink, then through a gateway to CompuServe. This is similar to the process that takes place when you get money from an automated teller machine that doesn't belong to your bank.

Of course, anyone who's not a member of a Telescript-based service doesn't get the full experience that a Magic Cap user gets. In other words, there's no room for animated kitty cats on traditional electronic mail. Messages usually get stripped down to just bare text when passing through gateways, but at least the essence gets transmitted. If you tell your friends and associates what they're missing, they'll have more incentive for getting a Magic Cap communicator.

Missing Link. There's a magical connection that lets most electronic mail services talk to each other: Internet. Almost every service, including PersonaLink, has a gateway to Internet, which is the sprawling worldwide web of computers that connects millions of users. Because most services can exchange mail through Internet, you can usually get mail from one place to another even if you and your recipient are on different services.

Groups

Magic Cap lets you associate groups of names together for easy communication. There are three built-in groups: Family, Friends, and Co-Workers, and you can add your own groups. After you've made a group, you can send a message to all the group's members at once, as we did in Chapter 2. This message can use different ways to get to each member: Some may be available on PersonaLink, others might have traditional electronic mail, and some slackers will only have fax machines.

Let's say you want to create a group for your department, and you've already entered name cards for the people you want to have in the group. Start by tapping *new* and then *group*, and then type *The Department* as the group's name. When you tap *done,* you'll see Figure 5-12, an empty group name card.

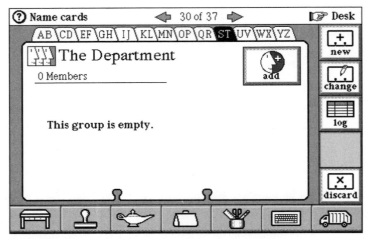

FIGURE 5-12.   Name card for newly added group

You can add members to the group by tapping *add*. The familiar name chooser appears, and you can pick a new group member and tap *accept*. When you do, the name chooser closes and the name you picked is added to the group. To add another, just tap *add* again and choose your next name.

If you're adding a bunch of group members at once, you might find it tedious to keep picking them out one at a time. A shortcut can help you here. As you tap *accept* to add the new group member, hold down the option key. This trick adds the member to the group, but leaves the name chooser open, ready for you to add someone else.

You can also use the group card to remove unwanted members from your group. To do this, tap the member you want to remove, then tap *remove*, and that member is outta there. If you're looking at the group and you want to see a member's name card, you can tap the member's name to select it and then tap *look up* to go directly to the member's name card.

Stamped Groups

There's another way to manage groups. To demonstrate it, we'll create a group that's a mailing list for Halloween cards (once you have electronic mail, you find yourself sending messages for all sorts of occasions). First, you make the new group by tapping *new*, then *group*, then typing *My Pumpkin Friends*, then *done*. Now, let's do something a little different: Tap the stamper, open the *occasions* drawer, and then slide the pumpkin stamp out and onto the image in the upper-left corner of the group card. The image slurps into place and becomes attached to the group.

Now you can add your friends Susan Anthony and Hans Anderson to the group. Tap *add*, choose Susan, tap *accept*, and then repeat the process for Hans (Figure 5-13). Go take a look at Susan's name card. When you do, you'll find that the pumpkin image has automatically been added to her card as a reminder that she's in the Halloween group.

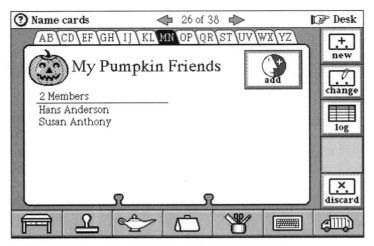

FIGURE 5-13. Name card for stamped group

This brings up an interesting question: What if you go to another name card and simply add a pumpkin stamp to the card? If you do just that, say on Mark Anthony's name card, and then go back to the *My Pumpkin Friends* group card, you'll see that you've added Mark Anthony to the group, just by dropping the appropriate stamp on his card. You can also remove members from the group the same way—just slide the group's stamp from the member's name card to the trash. So, when you associate a group with a stamp, you can add and remove group members simply by adding and removing the stamp.

Stamp of Approval. Here's a quick trick to add a bunch of members to a stamped group. Slide a copy of the group's stamp to the tote bag. Then, as you visit the card of each prospective member of the group, hold down the option key while you slide out of the tote bag. This will pull out a copy of the stamp, which you can then drop on the name card to add that name to the group.

The built-in groups, Family, Friends, and Co-Workers, work just like any other stamped groups. The Co-Workers group has one magic trick that the others don't have, though. When you make a new name card for a person whose company name is the same as yours, Magic Cap will automatically add the person to the Co-Workers group. If you don't really want the person in your Co-Workers group, you can slide the Co-Workers stamp off the name card and into the trash.

Customizing and Other Tricks

You can use any of the goodies from the stamp drawer or magic hat to decorate name cards, including sounds, songs, and animations, which is much tougher to do in a printed address book. If you see an image that reminds you of someone in your name card file, you can drop it in the upper-left corner of that person's name card and your custom image will replace the generic one.

There are a few other shortcuts in the name file to make it easier to move around. In addition to using the left and right arrows at the top of the screen to flip between cards, you can use option-right arrow to move to the last card or option-left arrow to move to the first .

If your communicator is plugged into a phone line, you can dial by tapping on the phone number on a name card. Magic Cap dials the number for you and shows you how long the call is taking. As we noted earlier, if you don't have a phone line connected, you can use the tones that come out of the communicator's speaker to dial a phone through its handset, although that trick doesn't work on all phones.

The commands in the lamp provide a few more handy goodies for the name file. Use the *find* command to search for names or stamps on name cards, *file* to store information on memory cards, and *print* to get your name cards on paper. When you file or print, you can choose all the cards in the file or just the one you're looking at.

Summary

The name file is a great address book, and it also helps you communicate with anyone listed there. You can add people, companies, and information services, and you can create groups for people who share something in common (such as family, friends, co-workers). There are lots of typing shortcuts built into the name file, since you'll spend a lot of time there entering information. Automatic completion of words is based on information that Magic Cap learns from previous entries, but it causes no harm if it guesses wrong. Automatic capitalization is another subtle trick that makes entering names easier.

A name card can handle people with single names (Cher), two first names with the same last name (Bill and Hillary Clinton), and business names (Upstairs Company) and it alphabetizes them correctly. If you enter a company name that your name file already knows, it will offer that company's work address and phone when you enter new employees of that company. Anything that's automatically entered shows up as selected text with the typing point properly placed, so you can type over it without extra work.

Stamps help you add additional information, letting you enter multiple addresses, phone numbers, fax numbers, and electronic mail addresses. The name file is available throughout Magic Cap, and you can access or add a new card while using the datebook, or phone, or stationery. The newest card you add, or the last one you viewed in the name file, becomes the current contact, and that name is highlighted in the name chooser window in any other scene. That name card remains the current contact when you are in the datebook (whom to schedule an appointment with), when you are using the phone (whom to call), or when you are composing mail (whom to address the message to).

You can log any communication (phone or mail) you have with anyone in your name file. You can get in touch with people who have mail addresses on other networks just by having their electronic address on their name card. If you receive mail from a client who's recently added a new fax number, the client's card in your name file will be updated. Similarly, any mail you send will have your name card attached, so the recipients of your messages can also be sure to have the most up-to-date information in their name files.

Chapter 6

 Phone

It's Your Call

Most of us started using telephones when we were very young, so our telephone habits were learned early in life, and they're very hard to change. When I was growing up, my mother only called people when she actually had something to tell them, and she didn't have much use for people who spent their time calling just to chat about stuff like what she made for dinner last night. My father, a doctor, obviously spent a lot of time on the telephone and later had a pager so that he could always be reached when he was on call.

These habits of my parents are probably where I get my feelings about the phone: Mostly, I find phones obtrusive and more often than not, I use an answering machine to screen my calls. Although I don't use the phone frivolously, I still have telephones around for convenience. I have phones in four different rooms at home, a separate line for my computer and even a portable cellular phone that moves from car to car. All these phones are around not necessarily because I want to be reachable anywhere, but because I want to be able to use the phone at my convenience; I want to be in touch. Although Magic Cap focuses on electronic mail, it also includes advanced, flexible telephone features, and these features can keep you in touch wherever you are.

Connected or Not

Tap the phone on the desk to use Magic Cap's phone features. The phone lets you do different sets of things depending on which of these three situations you're in:

1. Your communicator isn't connected to a telephone line.
2. Your communicator is connected to a telephone line.
3. Your communicator is connected to a telephone line and has a handset attached, or there's a telephone connected to the same line as your communicator.

In the first case, you can use the Magic Cap phone as an automatic dialer, playing touch tones into the mouthpiece of a standard telephone's handset to place a call. In the second case, you can use Magic Cap for one-way conversations where you only have to listen, not talk. The third case lets you use your communicator as a full telephone. We'll go over each of these three cases in this chapter's scenarios.

Keypad

You've probably already used the phone on the desk if you followed the *Getting Started* lessons. You went through a sequence of actions to tell your communicator your location to ensure that it dials properly, and you might even have made a phone call (see Chapter 1 if you need to refresh your memory). Since that might have been one of the very first things you did when you got your communicator, you may not have explored it fully. Let's go back to the phone and explain all the buttons and actions in some depth.

When you touch the phone, it opens to a scene that has a telephone keypad, buttons to help with dialing and saving phone numbers, a panel of blank speed-dial buttons, and a new set of buttons down the right side of the screen that controls your phone (see Figure 6-1). This is the keypad scene, and the top button on the right side, called *keypad*, is highlighted.

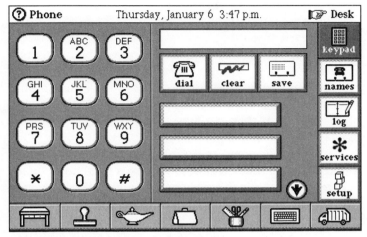

FIGURE 6-1. The phone's keypad

The most obvious thing to do with the phone is to make a call, as you did during the *Getting Started* lessons. Dialing the phone is easy—just press the digits on the keypad, and then touch *dial*. For flexibility, it also works the other way—touch *dial* to take the phone off the hook, and then dial the number.

If you have a communicator with an optional telephone handset, or there's a telephone connected to the same phone line, you can complete a call that lets you speak to the other party. Without the handset, you can hold the communicator up to the mouthpiece of a telephone so the tones will play and auto-dial the phone, although the communicator volume must be loud and the phone you're using has to be responsive to auto-dialing.

Let's say you dial directory assistance to get the telephone number of a popular new Italian restaurant. Instead of trying to find a pen and paper to jot the number down, or even using the notebook in your communicator and then having to manually dial the number, you can use the phone to cut out several steps. Tap the number on the keypad while you're getting it from directory assistance. There's a display that shows you the number as you're entering it, and it even formats it for you as you're typing it, properly separating the area code and prefix. Because you're entering it directly into Magic Cap's phone, you can then dial the number just by touching *dial*.

If you want to keep the number to use later, you can touch *save*, the button that looks like a little name card, and you'll get to make a new name card. You can choose to make the new card for a person or company. When you type in the name, you'll see that Magic Cap has already entered the phone number for you. The next time you feel like having lasagna, you'll have the name card of the restaurant and its phone number.

You might notice that *dial* changes to *hang up* after the call is made, so if the only available dinner reservations are before 4 or after 11, you can hang up and call somewhere else. After you hang up, that versatile button then becomes *redial* until you enter a new telephone number.

Whenever you dial a number, Magic Cap makes a *Phone status* window that tells you what number was dialed, and it lets you adjust the volume, see the log of phone calls, or hang up. You're not stuck in the phone scene after you've started a call; you can do other

actions, like opening the datebook to make an appointment or opening the call's log entry to take notes, all
while the phone call continues. When you switch scenes,
the *Phone status* window closes, but you can see it again
by touching the tiny telephone handset that appears at
the top of the screen while the call continues. When you're
ready to end the call, you can touch *hang up* in the *Phone
status* window.

You can also dial by touching any one of the nine speed-
dial buttons that you can program for your most frequent
calls. To set a speed-dial button, touch the blank button
to open it. You'll see a window (shown in Figure 6-2) that
lets you label the button and offers you a couple of choices
for how to enter the number.

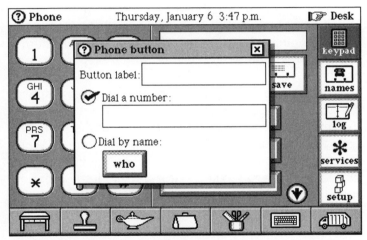

FIGURE 6-2. This window helps you program speed-dial
buttons

The *Dial by name* choice is probably the most common one for most numbers. If you're a concerned parent
as well as a full-time employee, you may want to have the

first button set for your home so you can check in with the nanny and make sure the little ones ate their lunches and took their naps. You can name the new button *Home*, check the *Dial by name* option, then touch *who* below it, which will produce a name chooser window that has a list of names. As in all name chooser windows, you can pick from the list, or you can touch *new* to make a new card and enter a name and phone number right then and there.

As you select the name you want (in this case, it will be your own), you will also see the phone number displayed above the *accept* button, as shown in Figure 6-3. If Magic Cap knows more than one phone number for the name shown, the numbers will appear in a choice box so you can scroll through and choose the right one. When you have the right combination of name and number, you can touch *accept* and you'll have a speed-dial button that will help you keep in touch with your kids, whether you're calling from your office or from a business trip in Boston.

You can also dial a number manually to set a speed-dial button. As soon as you touch the *Dial a number* box, the keyboard opens, already set to type numbers, and the typing point is placed so you can enter the number. When you're done entering the number, touch the *x* in the window to close it and the keyboard, and you'll see your new speed dial button set.

This is a handy feature for numbers you may call frequently that don't really have a person or company connected to them. An obvious speed-dial button you would set this way is 911, because it's unlikely you would want to enter a name card for that number. You might also want to set a speed-dial button this way for the local time and temperature phone numbers, or for a road conditions recording if you travel a lot.

146

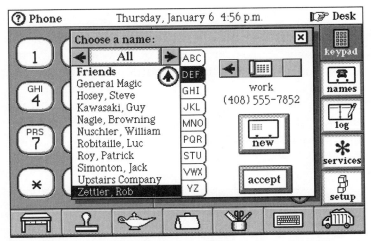

FIGURE 6-3. Speed dial's name chooser includes phone numbers

Once a speed-dial button is set, one simple touch on the button dials the number. You can reprogram a button by holding down the option key when you touch it. This tells Magic Cap that you want to change the button rather than use it to dial. Option-touching a programmed speed-dial button opens the window shown in Figure 6-2 to help you enter the new number.

Here's another Magic Cap shortcut: You don't have to label the button when you program it. If you touch a name card to get the phone number, and then close the window, the speed-dial button automatically takes its name from the name card, with the phone number's description added in parentheses. Similarly, if you program a button with just a number, the number will be used as the button's label.

Seeing Names and Logs

Because the phone is closely related to the name file, it makes sense to give you a quick way to view the name card list with all the phone numbers. When you touch *names*, a button with a picture of a telephone on a card, you see the familiar name chooser, but with one obvious difference: When you select a name from the list, you see all the phone numbers entered on that card with their accompanying stamps, as shown in Figure 6-4.

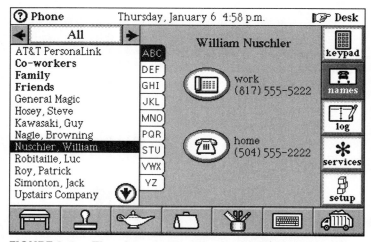

FIGURE 6-4. The phone's display of names and numbers

You can't open an individual name card from this index, but you can touch any phone stamp next to a name to dial the number. You might remember from Chapter 5 that when you're looking at a name card, you can touch the telephone stamps right on the name card to start dialing. This is exactly the same feature, except that you don't have to open the name file first.

The *log* button shows an index of the phone calls made from your communicator, as pictured in Figure 6-5. This can be especially useful if you contact a lot of clients by phone and you need to keep track of the calls for billing purposes. In fact, the first two rules that you can set for the phone involve logs. There's a rule that determines whether to make a log entry for each call, and another rule that automatically throws away old log entries after a certain amount of time has passed.

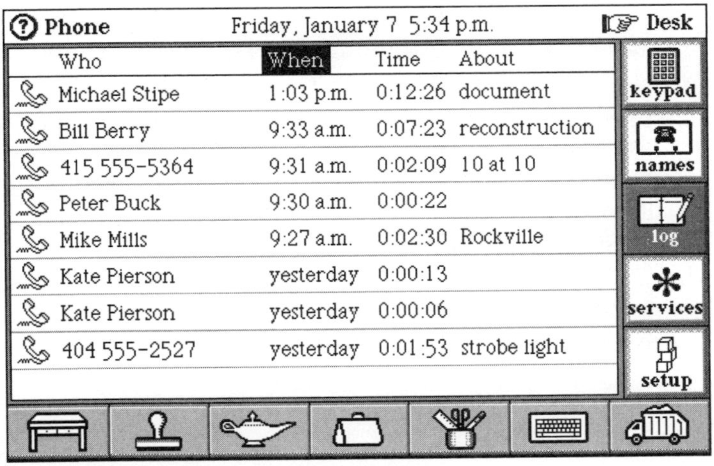

Who	When	Time	About
Michael Stipe	1:03 p.m.	0:12:26	document
Bill Berry	9:33 a.m.	0:07:23	reconstruction
415 555-5364	9:31 a.m.	0:02:09	10 at 10
Peter Buck	9:30 a.m.	0:00:22	
Mike Mills	9:27 a.m.	0:02:30	Rockville
Kate Pierson	yesterday	0:00:13	
Kate Pierson	yesterday	0:00:06	
404 555-2527	yesterday	0:01:53	strobe light

(?) Phone   Friday, January 7 5:34 p.m.   ☞ **Desk**

Desk panel: keypad, names, log, services, setup

FIGURE 6-5. The log of phone calls

The calls are logged according to the name or number called, depending on whether the number was chosen from the name card list or entered manually, and the log includes the time and duration of the phone call. If you look at the log on the same day you've made a call, you'll see the time that the call was started. If you look at the log anytime after that day, it will show the date of the call instead, making the log a much more useful tracking tool.

If you touch an individual entry in the log index, it zooms open to allow you to see the description of the call you wrote earlier, along with any notes you might have added regarding the call. You can also use stamps to mark the log entry, which you can then search for later. In consistent Magic Cap fashion, there are left and right arrows at the top of the log entry so you can move back and forth with ease. You'll get a log entry any time you call a number, whether you dial with the speed dial buttons, a manually entered number, or from a name in any of the phone's name lists. You'll also get a log entry when you dial a number by touching a phone number stamp while you're looking at a card in the name file.

You can have Magic Cap file your log entries in a folder in the file cabinet. You can file a log entry using the *file* command from the lamp, or by sliding an individual entry to the tote bag, opening the file cabinet, and then sliding the entry into a folder. If you spend a lot of your time on the phone with clients, you now have an easy way to track those minutes for billing purposes, because everyone wants a log.

Phone Rules

Let's explore the phone rules a little more. Besides the rules about making and keeping log entries, there are two rules about dealing with an incoming phone call. You probably won't be getting any phone calls unless you have a handset and a phone line connected to your communicator. (If you get an incoming phone call and you don't have a phone line connected, you're witnessing either a miracle or a spectacular bug.) You can set the rule that displays an announcement when any call is received, and you can choose a custom ring sound to alert you when a phone call comes in.

The last rule is vital for making sure that you can use your communicator in more than one place. As you take your communicator around, you'll connect and unplug it at different locations you've listed, which you might remember from the *Getting Started* lesson about telling the communicator where you're dialing from. The communicator needs to know where you are in order to dial calls correctly; if you call outside a number's area code, it must dial the area code first, of course.

To make this work properly, you'd have to remember to reset your location every time you connected in a different place. Of course, most people would forget to do this most of the time. To make this work better, a couple of dedicated engineers at General Magic thought it would be a good idea if the communicator could detect when you plugged into a phone line, so that whenever you connected, it would "feel the tickle" and remind you to tell it your location. After a lengthy struggle with communicator hardware, they were finally able to make this important feature work. If you leave the rule at its factory setting, the communicator will ask you to confirm your location each time it feels the tickle of a telephone line being plugged in. Figure 6-6 shows the message you see when you connect.

FIGURE 6-6. This window appears when you connect a phone line

Services

As we continue down the right side of the phone's screen, we see that the next button is called *services*. This takes you to a page that's intended to hold buttons to help you communicate with automated telephone response systems, such as voice mail, bank account balance inquiries, or stock quotations. However, the only thing you'll see when you touch this button is a page of text describing what you may be able to do soon with some third-party help.

Although Magic Cap doesn't come with any of these services built in, you can imagine what some of them might be. If your office has a voice-mail system, you know that you must press a specific sequence of numbers on the telephone keypad to get your messages. Because the communicator can play telephone tones, the communicator could be programmed to play the right tones when you touch buttons; for example, you could use a button labeled *save* instead of having to remember to dial 76 (or was it 67?) to save a message. A savvy phone company might offer you Magic Cap controls for your voice mail system on a memory card. You could insert the memory card and the page of commands would hop onto the *services* page.

You might also see information providers from downtown Magic Cap offer you similar services. If you're registered with the stock broker downtown, it might offer you a custom-programmed page of buttons that would step through the tones necessary to check on your personal portfolio of stocks using an automated attendant system. Finally, you'd have a release from the tyranny of those annoying automated instructions to "press 47, followed by the star key now."

Setting Up

The phone's *setup* page is one of the least intuitive places in Magic Cap, in part because it's not a metaphor for anything you have to do in real life. The main purpose of the phone setup is to tell the communicator where you are, something you usually don't have to do when you use a telephone. You've already seen the phone setup as part of the *Getting Started* lessons, but if you're like many of us, you may have followed the lesson without fully understanding what was happening and why.

You'll probably take your communicator to work, bring it home, take it with you on a business trip, and then use it at the airport when your flight is delayed. Because you work in different locations, your communicator needs to know where it is in case you ask it to dial the phone to collect your mail, call someone, or send a fax. You wouldn't have to do any of this if the telephone network allowed you to dial the area code you're in when you're calling another number in the same area. That way, you could always dial exactly the same digits to reach a number, no matter where you were (as long as you stayed in the same country).

Because the telephone network doesn't let you dial the area code when calling a local number, Magic Cap needs to know the area code you're in so it can dial out properly. That's why the gentle reminder to confirm where you are is so important.

When you first touch *setup*, you see the setup screen (shown in Figure 6-7) with the calling location you added in the *Getting Started* lessons. When you touch the stamper, a special phone drawer is opened, and you can choose from the images for home, work, and hotel. If you depend on your communicator at work, that might be the next stamp you add. After you touch the stamp for work, it hops onto the screen, a window for entering information opens, and the keyboard appears.

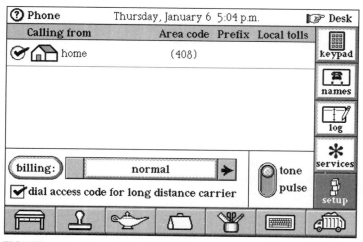

FIGURE 6-7. The phone's setup screen

The first step in the sequence is to type in the name of the location you're calling from. It already says *work*, but you can personalize it even more if you want, so we'll change it to say *office*. Next is a choice box with the country you're calling from, and as much as you'd like it to be Jamaica, you'll just keep it set to United States. Magic Cap then needs to know the area code you're calling from. Because many people live and work in different area codes these days, this may be the major difference between using your communicator at the office and at home.

Finally, you must tell your communicator if it needs to dial a prefix to get an outside line before calling. After you're done entering the location, you now have two items with check boxes that tell your communicator where it's calling from, as shown in Figure 6-8. When you connect to a phone line and the communicator asks you to confirm your location, you'll choose from these two options.

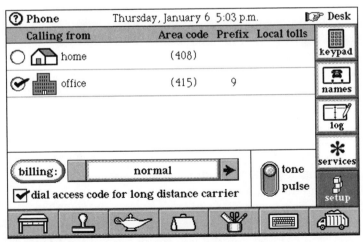

FIGURE 6-8. Phone setup now has *home* and *work* options

The stamper has choices for *work*, *home*, and *hotel*, but because you can enter a new name for these location stamps, you can make as many as you need. If you ever need to take your communicator on a trip to the Netherlands, you can add a new stamp for *hotel*, and set the country when you fill out the location. Magic Cap already knows most international calling codes, so when you connect to a phone line in Eindhoven, every one of your numbers on name cards will use the right country code as a prefix for dialing numbers back in the United States.

The other important part of the phone setup is the *billing* button, which is where you tell the phone how you're paying for long-distance calls. It comes factory set to *normal*, which means that no credit card information will be entered and the call will just be billed automatically to the caller (or the recipient, if you call collect). If you use a calling card or other credit card to keep track of phone expenses, or you want to connect to your own long-distance carrier, the *billing* button can help you.

You can tap *billing* to specify how to direct the charges, and there is also a place to enter a long-distance access code, if you want your communicator to dial that before calling a number. Magic Cap comes with several choices for credit cards, and you can change or remove them, or add your own to personalize your communicator to match your billing needs.

Magic Cap also comes with the access code to AT&T's long-distance service built in, but it can be easily changed to access any other carrier instead. There's a check box for telling the phone whether to dial the access code for your long distance carrier. If you've entered a new access code or just left it at the factory-set code for AT&T, it makes sense to keep this feature on. It doesn't get in the way of any dialing, and if you need it, you won't have to remember to keep turning it on and off. Finally, there's a switch to choose between tone and old-fashioned pulse dialing, if you happen to be plugged into a phone system that doesn't understand touch tones.

Summary

The main scene in the phone is the keypad. You can manually enter a phone number from the keypad and if you're connected to a phone line, the communicator can dial the phone for you with the touch of a button. The phone can help you even if you're not connected to a phone line or you don't have a telephone handset attached. Some models of communicators can be held up to the mouthpieces of some telephones, and the communicator can be used as an automatic dialer to initiate a call.

You can set numbers for nine speed-dial buttons, and you can either type in a number for these buttons or use the information already entered on your name cards to program them. The phone will let you save any manually entered number as a name card, without having to go to the name file. The names button is a fast way to see an index of all the names in your name file, and it displays the phone numbers entered on each card. You can quickly find any name and phone number this way, and you can start a call just by touching the stamp next to each number. When you make a call, you can move to another scene as the call continues.

The phone keeps a log of every phone call you make with your communicator, whether you touch a speed-dial button, manually enter a phone number, touch a phone number stamp from the names button in the phone, or touch a stamp in the name file itself. There is a log made of the time the call was made, who or what number was called, how long it lasted, and any notes you might have made.

The phone has rules about automatically making log entries and how long to keep them before discarding them. You can file individual log entries in your file cabinet if you need to keep them longer than the rule's limit.

You can look forward to filling the *services* scene with controls from software developers and information providers. These services help you use your communicator to control automated systems like voice mail, stock quotes, or ticket ordering.

The phone setup is one of the first things you do when you're personalizing your communicator, and you find out why it's important to tell your communicator where you're calling from. You can add entries for the different places you might be when you plug your communicator into a phone line. The phone knows how to dial from different area codes and countries, and it even includes long-distance carrier access codes and calling card numbers if you want. All you need to do is tell your communicator where it is, and it takes care of the rest.

 **Notebook**

A Blank Book

When I started to write about Magic Cap, I had very little trouble writing about the datebook, because I could easily see how to use Magic Cap instead of a printed calendar. The electronic mail information was a little intimidating because there was so much to tell, but the features there are well-designed and very important to Magic Cap. I was comfortable with the name file, easily understanding how Magic Cap's features could meet my needs for an address book, especially one that helps so much in actually communicating with people.

In contrast, I was really skeptical when I started to think about how I might use the notebook. I don't carry around a notebook, and I really couldn't see why I'd want to have one right on my Magic Cap desk. I was sure I'd have a hard time writing about something I didn't need or want to use. After a little experimenting, though, I saw how I might use it, and I found that I liked using it. I love getting nice surprises like that.

Writing it Down

When you open the notebook, you see a blank sheet of paper (see Figure 7-1) and all the promise that it brings. You can use this page just as you would use plain paper, with a few differences because the page only exists inside a personal communicator and not in the physical world.

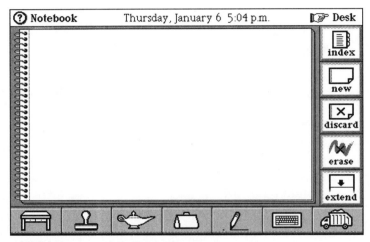

FIGURE 7-1. Blank notebook page

Magic Cap assumes that you'll want to write your notes rather than type them, so it automatically selects the pencil tool for you to write with. You can see which tool you're using by looking at the tool holder's space along the bottom of the screen. If you'd rather type, you can tap the keyboard to open the on-screen keyboard, but on plain paper, you'll probably want to jot down a quick note or make a simple drawing with your stylus.

You can choose pencils that have different points for writing, depending on how thick you want your lines. If you're writing a note to remind yourself that you have to call your associate in Salt Lake City, you'll probably be content with the thin pencil that the notebook gives you when the new page opens. If you're drawing a map to your house for friends who are coming to dinner from out of town, you might use a thicker pencil to show busier roads.

Bucking a trend in personal electronics, Magic Cap communicators don't try to recognize your handwriting. The notebook doesn't try to interpret the notes you write, instead giving you this choice: You can use a pencil to convey the personal touch of handwriting, or you can use the keyboard to type in text that must be entered with precision. Using a stylus to write on a screen takes some practice—you have to get used to how fast to move and how hard to press. Once you get the hang of it, though, it's fun and easy.

Mapping the Way

Many folks are not great artists and admit to needing all the help they can get with drawing. Magic Cap provides tools for shapes and lines that will help your drawings look much more presentable. Let's assume you want to draw a map to your office for a visiting customer. Start by drawing the lines for Highway 280 and Highway 17 freehand with a pencil, since roads are rarely straight lines anyway. You can tap the tool holder to see a list of choices that includes lines and shapes; you'll use these shortly to help draw other things.

As you start drawing the freeway exit that leads to your office, you discover a mistake: You didn't leave enough room to write the details of finding your office after getting off the freeway. This gives you a chance to try out the *erase* button on the right side of the screen.

Tapping *erase* removes the marks on the page one at a time, the most recently added ones first. You can also pick the eraser from among the pencil tools and use your stylus or finger like an eraser, rubbing over just the marks you want to erase (see Figure 7-2).

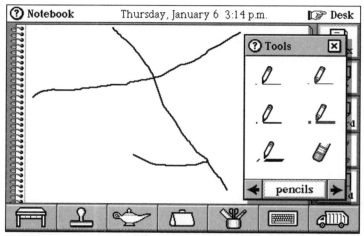

FIGURE 7-2. Part of the map

If you want, you can skip the erasing and tap *discard* to get rid of this page and start over again (and again, and again, if you want). The *discard* command tears the page out of the notebook and throws it away. To begin again, you can tap *new* and then choose the kind of paper for the new page from among the notebook's six kinds of stationery (see Figure 7-3).

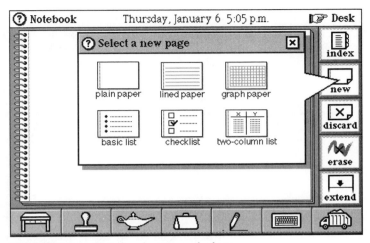

FIGURE 7-3. Notebook paper choices

If you're working on a notebook page and you want to start over, you don't have to throw the page away or pick a new one. Here's the shortcut for starting over on a page: If you hold down the option key and tap *erase*, all the pencil marks, stamps, lines, and other customizations on the page are erased at once, leaving you once again with a blank piece of paper. Think of it as recycling.

Lines and Words

If you're one of the many who can't draw a straight line unless you're using a ruler (and with me, even that's no guarantee), you'll appreciate Magic Cap's line tools. These tools let you draw straight lines of different thicknesses and at various angles. They're represented by lines in the tool holder, which you can use to draw both horizontal and vertical lines. These tools are different from the pencils because they guarantee straight lines. In fact, there are line tools that produce two different kinds of lines: lines that can be drawn at any angle, and lines that always snap to the nearest 90-degree angle. You can see the line tools in Figure 7-4.

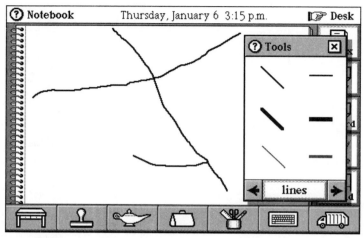

FIGURE 7-4. Line tools

After working on the map awhile, you might realize that you'd also like to give the directions in words; even with Magic Cap, drawing a legible map is kind of a chore. Now you can use the text tools in the tool holder to make a new text field on the notebook page. Tap the tool holder and then go to the text tools. Tap *plain* to make a text field that will show its contents with a simple line around it as a border, which will be ideal for the map's title.

When you choose the plain text field, its image hops into the tool holder, showing the tool that you're using. Then, when you tap the page, a new field is placed at the touch point, the keyboard opens, and you can start typing. When you're done, you can tap the tool holder again to make another text field. This time, you can pick *transparent*, which will show the typed text with no border at all. Transparent text fields are ideal for written directions on a map that can blend in with the drawing.

If you want to dress up the map you're making, you might go for a *fancy* text field, which borders its words with a more elegant frame. Every time you pick a different text field, the text choices window disappears and the image hops into the tool holder. If you want to go back and edit your text after entering it, just tap directly on the words. As shown in Figure 7-5, Magic Cap opens the text selection window, which lets you retype the text, change its style, copy it, or remove it.

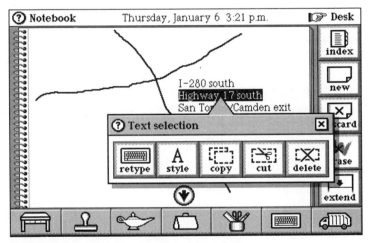

FIGURE 7-5. Selected text opens window

Arrangements

The last set of tools is for arranging items on a page. If you tap *move*, which has an image that looks something like a moving van without wheels but on closer inspection is a box with motion lines, you can slide any object that you've placed on the page. This comes in handy when you realize the written directions cover up part of the freeway on the map.

With the *copy* tool, you can duplicate any item and slide it to another position on the page or stash it in the tote bag to put on another page. This can be useful for reusing pieces of a drawing, such as changing a map for someone coming from a different direction. You can even copy the text and then change it to make it applicable to the other person's starting point. You can use *stretch* to reshape any item you've put on the page, so when you figure out that the exit off the freeway doesn't really look the way you drew it, you can make the line longer or shorter instead of drawing it again.

Evolution.   In the early development of Magic Cap, the *move*, *copy*, and *stretch* tools were far more important. Before there was a notebook or datebook, Magic Cap's features consisted mainly of construction tools for assembling components. In that world, the arranging tools were vital. In fact, they were so important that at one point, each of those tools was assigned its own physical key on the communicator's case. Eventually, the designers found a way to avoid the need for the arranging tools most of the time, and the dedicated keys were removed.

Send It Off

After you've created a notebook page by drawing or writing, you can actually use what you've made to communicate with someone. As long as you've gone to the trouble to draw the map, you should probably make sure your guest sees it before coming. With just a touch of the lamp, you can send the message by tapping *fax*—there goes one excuse for arriving late at your office (see Figure 7-6).

FIGURE 7-6. Preparing to fax the map

You can choose to send the page you just made or a picture of the whole screen, and the *options* button lets you decide whether to include a cover page and whether to have the fax come out sideways. You can tap *to:* and pick the addressee you want with the name chooser. If your addressee is already in the list, you can choose the name, and then tap *send fax* to get the fax going. If you haven't yet added the addressee to the name file, you can add a new name card and fill in the fax number in the same step, without ever leaving the notebook. (Of course, when you open the name file, the name you just entered will appear because it's the current contact, and you'll be able to add addresses and more phone numbers if you want to, but you probably already guessed that).

By faxing the map right away, your customer can get it before leaving work, and then you won't have to worry about playing telephone tag or dictating the directions over the phone.

A Birthday Card

A blank piece of paper just begs for a child's creativity. Let's say you're helping Jess, an imaginative eight-year-old who wants to use your communicator to make a birthday card for his grandmother (coincidentally, she just got her first personal communicator, too). The *shapes* tools in the tool holder let him pick from various kinds of shapes, including circles, stars, rectangles, and more (see Figure 7-7).

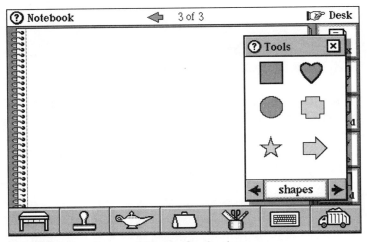

FIGURE 7-7.   Some of Magic Cap's shapes

After selecting the heart by tapping it, the heart shape hops into the tool holder, and you can show your young artist how to draw hearts all over the page. We'll stick with hearts right now, but by option-tapping the heart in the tool holder spot, the shapes choices reappear, making the other shapes available.

After choosing the heart shape as the tool of choice, Jess can touch the screen wherever he wants to put the shape and then slide to stretch the shape to any size and proportion. When he makes an arrow shape, it points to the right or left depending on which way he slides. He can go to the text tools, and then choose a fancy text field and place it on the screen. As the field is placed, the keyboard appears, and he can type a happy birthday message.

Just a plain *Happy Birthday, Bubbie!* isn't good enough for an eight-year-old, of course. He wants to make the words appear bigger and bolder. To do this, he slides through the words, which selects them and opens the text selection window (see Figure 7-8). Then, he can change the type face (there's a sample that shows what each choice will look like), the type size (he likes 18 point), and the style (he'll choose from bold, italic, or underline). Naturally, he thinks he wants bold, italic, *and* underline, but ultimately he decides that bold by itself looks coolest.

Next, he chooses the pencil tool so he can sign his name. Third-graders are still working on spacing and he runs out of room for his elaborate signature. But Magic Cap saves him: he taps *extend*, and the page grows by about half. Now there's plenty of room to finish signing. He's ready to finish decorating the card, so he taps the stamper to see what's inside. With the stamper open, he can adorn the card with as many stamps as an eight-year-old can hope for (which is a lot).

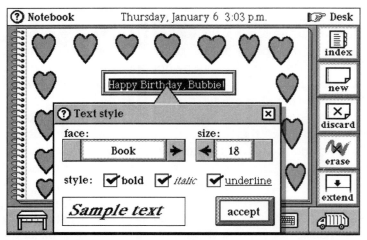

FIGURE 7-8. Eight-year-olds don't know from subtlety

Of course, Jess can't resist the animated birthday candle holding a piece of cake, and he drops a song stamp on the candle to make it play a catchy tune as it dances back and forth across the bottom of the card. At last, the card is ready to be sent. Jess touches the lamp, then *mail*, and then the *send* button. He chooses his grandmother's name from the list, and Magic Cap makes a new message for her and attaches the notebook page birthday card.

The card goes off with a tap of *send*, and the next time his grandmother checks her mail, she'll see a message from Jess. When she touches the notebook page that's attached, she'll see an original drawing from her grandson that moves and plays music. And she'll have a very, very happy birthday.

Notebook Index

As you look down the right side of the screen, you'll see the commands for pages in the notebook: *index*, *new*, *discard*, *erase*, and *extend*. All of these are similar to commands in other parts of Magic Cap, but a couple of them have special twists just for the notebook.

As in other parts of Magic Cap, the top of the screen shows the total number of pages and which page is currently showing, as well as left and right arrows for flipping through the pages. While you're looking at any page in the notebook, you can tap *index* and you'll get a pictorial table of contents for the notebook. You'll see miniature versions of every page, as in Figure 7-9.

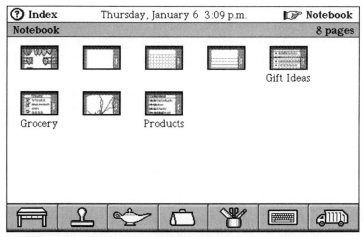

FIGURE 7-9. Notebook index shows miniature cards

You can use the index to get to any page that's displayed. Just tap on a miniature image of a page and you'll go there. There's more to do with the index. You can also slide these miniature pages to the tote bag and then attach them to messages as enclosures—they take the full-size version along, too. We'll look at an example of how you might do that.

While you're in a staff meeting, you might take notes for your upcoming trip to a trade show. Later, after the meeting ends, you can tap *index* and see miniature images of each page in the notebook. Slide the page of notes to the tote bag. You can also option-slide the image, which would ask Magic Cap to make a copy of the page to go into the tote bag, leaving the original in the notebook.

Then, you open the datebook and make a new multi-day appointment for the trade show trip. Once that's done, you can slide the miniature notebook page out of the tote bag and onto the business trip appointment. That's all you have to do to attach your notes to the appointment. By tapping the notebook page, you can take a look at the notes to make sure you have everything ready for the trip. By attaching it to the appointment for the business trip, you can find the notes the next time you have to travel on business. You can even edit the notes without leaving the datebook, thanks to smart integration of information in Magic Cap.

Consistency in the Interface. Consistency is a Magic Cap standard, and when you see things that look the same in Magic Cap, you can guess that they'll probably work the same way, too. In the name file or in box, you can option-tap the right arrow to see the last card, or option-tap the left arrow to see the first card. If you try the same trick in the notebook, you get the same result: option-tap the right arrow to flip to the last page in the notebook, and option-tap the left arrow to go back to page one.

Drawing on Paper

Not everybody likes to start out with a blank piece of paper staring them in the face. Some folks feel more comfortable with lined paper, and the notebook lets you work on paper that has lines on it, like school paper. If you type on lined paper, the words fit nicely between the lines. Of course, the words automatically wrap to the next line if they don't fit (and you might actually remember back when *that* was magic). Although the lines are kind of narrow for writing a lot of legible text, you might imagine a future version of Magic Cap that lets you choose between college rule and wide rule.

You might think of charts and graphs as business tools, but that eight-year-old who sent the birthday card to his grandmother probably makes a lot of little graphs in school. Students use graphs to help them visualize their estimates of things, like the total number of letters in the names of the students in the class. Before planting their garden, they need to make a line graph of the temperatures over a period of three school weeks to determine if the time is right to plant certain seeds.

The notebook provides two kinds of paper to help with this: lined paper, which has horizontal lines, and graph paper, which comes with a grid on it. Yes, you may have thought it was just a communicator, but it's also a notebook! It's a datebook! It's a learning tool! It slices and dices! But wait, there's more!

Let's start with a sheet of graph paper. To make a graph of temperatures, you start by choosing the horizontal line tool from the tool holder so you can make the axes. The horizontal axis needs to cover 15 lines for each day of the three school weeks. The vertical axis should probably have at least 20 lines (each line will be two degrees), in case you need to cover a spring cold spell.

When you try to put 20 vertical lines on a page, you'll quickly see that they won't fit. To get more space on the page, just tap *extend* and you'll get more lines at the bottom of the page. Go to the arranging tools and tap *stretch*, and you can extend the vertical axis to cover 20 lines. That just about runs to the bottom of the extended page, so you can tap *extend* again to get some room at the bottom for labels. The grid is complete now; you can see a screenful of it in Figure 7-10.

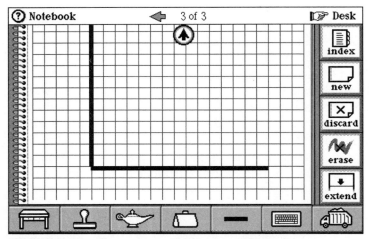

FIGURE 7-10. Temperature grid on graph paper

Now you can open the text tools and choose *transparent* to add labels for days under the horizontal axis. The vertical axis is next, and after that's done, you can start recording the temperatures using circles (from the shape tools). To start going in circles, tap the tool holder, get to shapes, and then tap the circle and see it hop into the tool holder. You can then touch the places on the screen that represent the temperatures for each of the 15 days. Your typical kid will really love this part; in fact, it'll take great restraint to prevent going crazy touching the screen and putting circles everywhere.

Should you connect all the points on the graph with lines? If you're not sure, try it; you can erase them if you don't like them. Use the tool holder to choose a line tool, which draws straight lines at any angle. Then go ahead and connect the dots, another big hit with the eight-year-old meteorologist crowd. After you finish drawing the lines, your young collaborator may decide it looked better before you added the lines, so you can have a great time pressing *erase* over and over as you watch each line disappear while making the trash noise. After you're sure the graph is done, if you're connected to a printer you can tap the lamp and print the page. If you don't have a printer connected, you can get a paper copy by faxing the page to a fax machine in your home or office. You and your favorite eight-year-old will have learned the valuable skill of making a line graph, and the planting season will no doubt be a great success.

Gifts and Groceries

You'll find list-making paper available in the notebook. To get a page of lined paper with a circle marking each item, tap *new* and then *basic list*. If you like making lists, you might read through your favorite holiday catalog and use a basic list to enter the goodies that you'd really like to convince someone to get for you.

When you tap a line item on a list page, the keyboard opens so you can type its name. You can tap *return* to move to the next line to type in the next item. Once you've entered several items in the list, you can alphabetize them by using the *sort* button in the lamp. But you realize that alphabetizing them really doesn't convey the proper order of how much you want each one (hint, hint, wink, wink), so you can rearrange the list to suit your priorities just by touching an item and sliding it to the position you want. When you do this, the item moves into the desired position and everything else automatically moves down a line.

If you decide to take something off your list (you realize that you've already got one, and one is plenty), you can throw it away by sliding it out of the list and into the trash. When you do, every other entry moves up, so there won't be a glaring empty line in the middle of your list.

If you want to change something, you can go back and edit an item just by touching that line. When you do that, Magic Cap opens the keyboard again and selects the text, giving you a chance to retype or add anything to the item. If you really want to push your luck, you can even tap *extend* to make room for more stuff on the page. See Figure 7-11 for the example list.

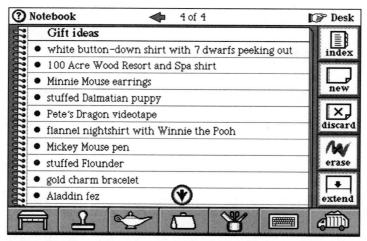

FIGURE 7-11. Gifts from favorite catalog

You might make other lists that are slightly more mundane, like what to buy on the weekly trip to the grocery store. The notebook provides checklist stationery, which, as the clever name implies, gives you lined paper and starts each line with a check box that you can tap to make a check mark. When you make a shopping list, you probably think of what you need to buy when someone in your family finishes the box/can/bag/bottle. It would be great if you could list the items according to the aisles in the store, but let's not get carried away.

If you list the items you need to pick up before leaving home, you can take your communicator to the store and when you actually take something off the shelf, you can tap the item's check box so you'll know the item is in the cart. When you get the lunch meat and cheese (they're in the same aisle), you can check each one individually even though they're separated by four other items, and then proceed to the next aisle for taco shells and seasonings. You can always extend the page if you need a bigger list. Figure 7-12 shows the example checklist.

If there are still some items left on your list after the shopping is done (let's say they were out of garlic bagels and the bananas were too ripe), you can slide the checked items into the trash, leaving the first two items on the checklist for your next shopping trip. Now that you've got just the two remaining items, you can do some fancy Magic Cap tricks to keep your shopping organized.

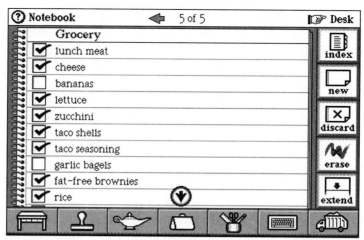

FIGURE 7-12. Grocery checklist

First, you can tap *index* to see the miniature images of your notebook pages. You locate the grocery checklist and slide it into the tote bag. Stepping back to the desk, you open the datebook and enter a *to do* appointment for going to the grocery store (a different one) tomorrow. Slide the miniature notebook page out of the tote bag onto the appointment and tap *save*. When you go to the grocery store tomorrow, you'll find the shopping list attached to that appointment. You can open and work with the checklist right in the datebook. You can check any of the boxes or throw away items. If you want, you can add other items to the list as you think of them.

Taking Snapshots. You can make your own versions of those miniature images in any part of Magic Cap. If you have construction mode turned on (see Chapter 10 to learn how), you'll find a camera in the lamp that takes snapshots. These snapshots are reduced versions of whatever scene you're in. You can drag the snapshot to other scenes; then, when you touch the snapshot, you'll be transported to the scene in the snapshot.

Because you made a *to do* appointment, it will appear on today's page in your datebook until you complete it. You can even take the list back to the notebook and reinsert it there, just as if you had a three-ring binder. You could also slide the image back into the tote bag and carry it back to the notebook. Because you've got your communicator with you all the time, you can add items to it whenever you think of them. That includes important work revelations that come to you at home as well as must-buy grocery items that you think of when you're at work.

Two-Column Lists

The Magic Cap notebook has another kind of list, which provides two columns of information. This list would be useful, for example, if you were brainstorming to make a list of your company's proposed new products and prices. Start by tapping *new*, then *two-column list* to make a new page. You can touch the top of the first column and rename it by typing *Products*. You rename the other column the same way, calling it *Prices*.

Each line starts with the same circle that appears on the basic list. When you tap an item, the keyboard opens so you can type the product's name. After you type an item, you touch *return* to move to the price column, where you can decide how much to price the product. Another tap on *return* and you're on the next line, ready for another product. You can see the two-column list in Figure 7-13.

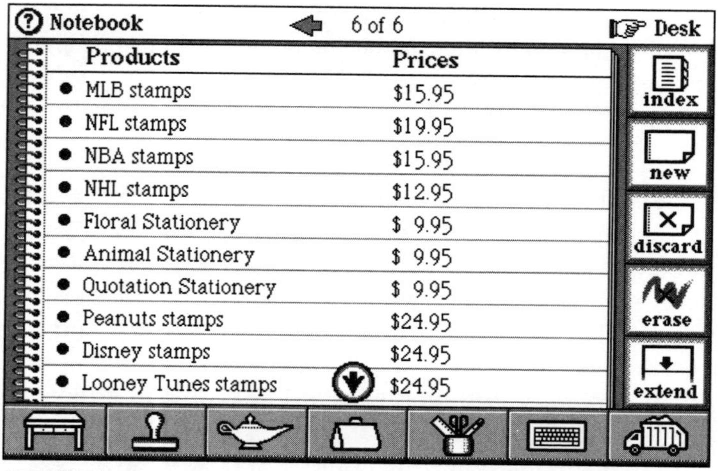

Products	Prices	
● MLB stamps	$15.95	index
● NFL stamps	$19.95	
● NBA stamps	$15.95	new
● NHL stamps	$12.95	
● Floral Stationery	$ 9.95	discard
● Animal Stationery	$ 9.95	
● Quotation Stationery	$ 9.95	erase
● Peanuts stamps	$24.95	
● Disney stamps	$24.95	extend
● Looney Tunes stamps	$24.95	

FIGURE 7-13. Two-column list of products and prices

You can slide a product to move it, and when you do, the corresponding price in the second column goes with it. You can tap *sort* in the lamp to alphabetize the products. When you alphabetize, the prices follow along with the products, of course. A handy feature in a future version of Magic Cap would let you sort the second column so you could see the products listed from the cheapest to the most expensive.

Customizing

One of the ways that Magic Cap helps you work is by letting you customize features that you use frequently. You can make your own kinds of appointments in the datebook, design your own stationery for sending messages, or add your own forms to the notebook. Let's make a new custom form now.

If you're an avid fan of a popular sports team, you might find yourself in the position of buying full season tickets but not attending all the games. If you're often in the position of trying to sell extra seats (where permitted by law, of course), you might like to have a quick and easy way to advertise the games you want to sell. The seat location and the price don't change from game to game, and the information about how to reach you also stays the same. The only thing that does change, then, is the date of the game and the opponent (for example, if you're a National League baseball fan who doesn't live in New York, you may have lots of games available against the Mets).

To make the new form, start by tapping *new*, and because the new form will be mostly text, tap *plain paper*. You can use the keyboard to type the information that's always the same. When you've entered that stuff, you can spruce up the page a bit by making a boldface headline to draw attention to it. You've already seen how to edit text: Slide across the sentence, which selects the text and opens the text selection window. Tap *style*, *bold*, size *18*, and then *accept*.

When you've finished designing the advertisement, you're ready to make it into a form. Tap *index* to see a miniature image of the page, and then slide it into the tote bag. Go back to the notebook view by tapping the step-back hand or *Notebook* in the upper-right corner. Tap *new* to see the *Select a new page* window, and then slide the miniature page out of the tote bag and into the window. The new page pops into place, and your newly designed form is added to the choices for new pages.

As a final touch, you can give your new form a descriptive name. Option-tap the keyboard image to open the keyboard with label maker. Type the new name (*Tix for sale*), slide the label right onto the new form, and the paper is renamed (see Figure 7-14). From now on, whenever you want to try to sell your tickets, you've already got the right form in your notebook. Let's hope they have a great season!

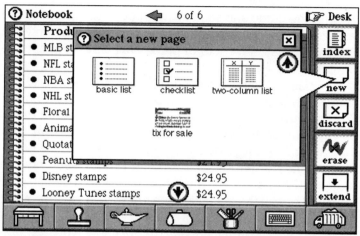

FIGURE 7-14.   Custom form added to notebook

Summary

The notebook is the place for writing and drawing freehand, as well as typing notes that are not necessarily going to be seen by anyone else. The notebook paper doesn't try to interpret your handwriting, so you can jot down notes or type them. You can use built-in writing and drawing tools, like pencils and lines of different thicknesses and several different shapes.

The notebook pages can be plain paper, lists, lined paper, or graph paper, and you can easily extend any kind to make longer pages. You can stamp any kind of paper with anything you find in the stamp drawer. You can add music, sound effects, and animations to your notes. There's an erase button that removes marks you've made. There's also an eraser tool that you can use with your finger or stylus that simulates rubbing with the eraser at the end of a pencil.

You can use the keyboard to type anything on the notebook paper, and you can even specify the kinds of border (or no border) that encloses the text. There are tools to arrange the items on your paper: *stretch* lets you extend lines and shapes that have already been drawn, *copy* lets you duplicate things for use on other pages or elsewhere in Magic Cap, and *move* lets you slide objects around on the page.

There's an index in the notebook that shows miniature images of each page. You can move these miniature images around to use elsewhere. You can slide one into the tote bag, and then slide it out onto an appointment in your datebook. It remains an active, editable page, even inside the datebook. You can also attach a notebook page to a message that you want to send.

Because you can always use *mail* and *fax* in the lamp, you can touch *mail* when you're looking at a notebook page and it will shrink and hop onto a postcard, ready for you to address and send. You can also choose to fax it, with an option to add a cover page or to turn it sideways. To fully customize your notebook, you can design your own kind of paper and then add this new form to the choices that are available whenever you add a new page to your notebook.

Chapter 8

File Cabinet

Filing

I hate to file. Sure, I love to buy filing paraphernalia—folders, color-coded labels, storage boxes of all shapes and sizes. I have every intention of being able to find all the insurance records when I need them, keeping the frequent flier mileage statements where they belong, and knowing where to track down the Little League roster, the third-grade class list, and every other phone list I have. You know what they say about good intentions and a certain road, though. I hate to file.

Machines do not hate to file. In fact, that's one of the things they do best. People who in real life are allergic to manila are often not very thorough about filing things on their computers, either. For them, filing means selecting an image and dragging it into another image. It's hard to find the time to set up an efficient filing system, so everything winds up in folders named *Filed stuff #37* and so on.

Magic Cap's designers recognized that filing shouldn't have to take much time, thought, or effort. A good set of filing features should be flexible enough to accommodate various styles of filing behavior, from those who just want to stash things quickly to folks who set up elaborate systems for putting everything away. Well-designed filing features should include built-in shortcuts and commands to file things automatically and have them end up where users expect them.

In the File Cabinet

Tucked behind the desk on the right side is the file cabinet. When you touch it, it opens to show you a drawer inside, which you can see in Figure 8-1. The drawer is filled with neat rows of folders, with the folders' left, right, and center index tabs lining up perfectly, another one of those things that never works out in the physical world. Magic Cap's file cabinet guesses that most of the things you'll file will be electronic mail messages that you've received or sent, so it has built in drawers for each of those two categories.

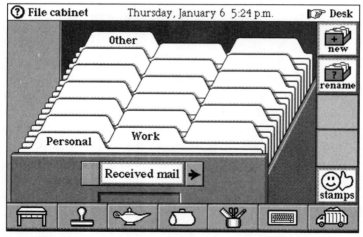

FIGURE 8-1. *Received mail* drawer in file cabinet

You can also create whole new drawers for more specific subjects, and every drawer has 19 folders that you can fill with information. Although you'll usually file messages here, you can actually use the file cabinet to hold onto several different kinds of items, including notebook pages, name cards, and old appointments.

Drawers in real file cabinets usually have a small paper label that shows what's kept inside, just above each drawer handle (a legendary story says that author L. Frank Baum spotted the bottom drawer of his file cabinet when trying to decide what to call the fantasy city in his children's story, and the Land of Oz got its name). In the Magic Cap file cabinet, that space also contains a choice box that you can use to choose which drawer you want to see.

The choice box has the familiar left and right arrows to show you its choices. Touching the label itself opens up a window that lists all the available drawers, and you can open the desired drawer just by touching any of the names on that list. If you add more drawers, you can take advantage of these consistent shortcuts: Option-touch the right arrow to see the last choice, or option-touch the left arrow to see the first choice.

Building a New Drawer

Let's say you're a real estate agent, and you want a drawer to keep notes about the different properties you have listed. Each house could have its own folder, which might contain some messages you sent to confirm some details of the property, messages you received from prospective buyers, and any notes you may have made about the features of that house. You may even want to keep copies of the name cards of prospective buyers in the folders.

If you needed more space for a real file cabinet in your office, you'd go and buy a new one. It's much easier to add another drawer to the Magic Cap file cabinet—just touch *new* in its familiar top spot on the right side of the screen. The keyboard opens, along with a window where you can type the name for the new drawer, which we'll call *Properties* (see Figure 8-2). *Properties* then pops in as the drawer's name, and it's also added to the choice box as the last choice.

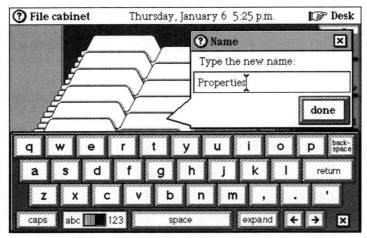

FIGURE 8-2. Making new *Properties* drawer

If you find that you've made a mistake in typing the name of the drawer, or if you want to change the name entirely, you can tap *rename* to get the keyboard and the naming window again. If you decide you want to get rid of the whole drawer and anything you may have filed there, you can tap *discard* and the drawer will be gone. You can get rid of any drawers you create, but the *Received mail* and *Sent mail* drawers are bolted in there permanently and can't be removed.

Once you've built the drawer, naming the folders inside it is also intuitively simple: You just touch the index tab at the top of a folder. When you do, the folder opens, the keyboard appears, and the typing point is positioned at the center of the index tab, as shown in Figure 8-3. Folder names are limited to the available width of a folder tab (about 10 characters), so you might just use the street name of each house in the example.

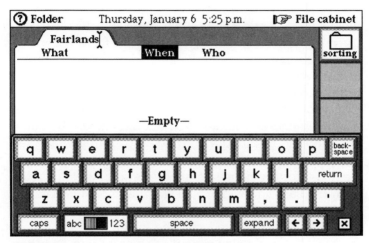

FIGURE 8-3. Typing a name for the folder

Because you get to decide which folders to name, you can put them in any order in the drawer. Once you've named the folders, you can reposition them by sliding them around in the drawer. If you've just recently created a *Fairlands* folder named after a street, you may want to move it so it's alphabetically in front of the *Hacienda* property folder, but behind the *Capri* townhouse folder.

As you're sliding *Fairlands*, you can see a ghostly outline of the folder and its label as it travels across the drawer, and you can even see the other folders move out of the way as you slide past them. When you get to the desired spot, you can stop sliding as it snaps into place. Of course, you can put the folders in any order you're comfortable with—alphabetically, chronologically in order of when you listed the property, in order of asking price, or anything else you want. An interesting enhancement for a future version of Magic Cap would be to include a way to automatically alphabetize the folders.

Once you have items filed inside a folder, you can move the filed items from one place to another just by sliding them. Let's say that Mr. and Mrs. Rusanowsky are prospective home buyers and you have a copy of their name card in the Fairlands folder. If they're unimpressed with that property, you'd like to move their name card to another house you think they might like.

To move their name card, tap the folder tab to open the folder, choose the item you want to move (the name card) and slide it into the tote bag. Tap *File cabinet* to see all the drawers again, and then slide the name card into the folder for the house on another street, which should be in the same drawer. You'll see the ghost and label of the Rusanowskys' name card as you're moving it, and you'll hear it get sucked into the folder where you now want it. You could also slide it to the tote bag and then move it to a new drawer, or even slide it into the trash if they've finally decided to leave town altogether.

File folders also give you a shortcut that lets you pull items out without even opening the folders. While you're looking at a file cabinet drawer, touch a folder tab and slide; the first thing you filed in the drawer pops out and comes along wherever you drag it, and you see its image and label as you drag. You can then drop it somewhere else, such as in another folder, the tote bag, or the trash.

Moving Folders

You can move whole folders and their contents to different drawers. If the real estate business is slow, you might need to add a drawer called *Inactive*, for properties that haven't sold in several months. For example, if the folder for the Hacienda property is empty because you've had no interest from anyone, you might want to move it to the *Inactive* drawer.

To move the folder, start by sliding it into the tote bag, opening the other drawer, and then pulling the folder out of the bag and into the new drawer. As you slide the folder, you'll see the outline of the folder and its label moving along the screen and into the tote bag; you'll leave an empty, unnamed folder behind in its place. Next, use the choice box to open the *Inactive* drawer. Then you can slide the folder back out of the tote bag into the new drawer and drop it into whichever position you want.

If you're a successful real estate agent, you'll probably want to add another new drawer called *Sold*. After the Fairlands property sells, you may want to move that folder and its information to the new drawer. To move an empty folder between drawers, you only need to slide it in and out of the tote bag. Magic Cap requires that you hold down the option key when there are things in the folder so it can tell that you want to drag the whole folder and not just something inside.

After you've got the folder in the tote bag, you can switch to a different drawer or create a new one; then you can slide the folder out of the tote bag and into the *Sold* drawer, with all its contents intact. Magic Cap always shows you how many items are in a folder because each time you add or remove something, a number just to the left of the folder name changes to reflect how many items are filed there.

Sorting Incoming Mail

Because Magic Cap was designed around easy communication, the file cabinet was built to automatically file incoming and outgoing messages. In Chapter 2, we discussed rules for the in box and out box about filing messages with certain text, senders, or even stamps. By using these rules, you can have the in box file your incoming messages in folders you specify before you even read them.

If you're an account executive for a sporting goods company, you have to sell lots of different items to various retail stores. Because you're on the road a lot, it makes sense for your customers to send their orders to you via electronic mail, rather than take their chances reaching you by phone. One of your biggest customers, Barry B's Baseball World, is having a sale on catchers' equipment, so the manager needs to add to his regular order. Soccer Locker is running low on shin guards and will need more before your next visit. In addition to those orders, you get regular orders from Hockey Hut and What A Racket!, as well as sales reports and messages from the main office.

You can set up a folder for each store in the drawer for *Received mail*. Then, you can set rules for your in box to look at the senders of each message you receive and file it in the appropriate folder before you even open the messages. If you make a folder for each store, then messages from Barry B's will be filed automatically in that store's folder, and so on.

When you create folders for senders and direct your inbound mail to go there by setting the appropriate in box rules, your mail is presorted and it's already categorized when you read it. If you don't specify where to file the messages from other senders, they'll stay in the in box until you read them or file them another way. For more information on using the in box rules to file messages, take another look at Chapter 2.

Filing Messages Manually

Some people feel a bit uneasy having their unread mail shuffled off to a folder as soon as it arrives in the in box. These folks like to work from the in box, knowing that messages get filed only after they've been read. If a message must be forwarded, or if it needs a reply, or even if it should be thrown away, they prefer to direct the action themselves instead of having instructions that are carried out by magic.

If you use your communicator to answer customer service questions, you might want to make sure that each message gets personal attention. You can leave the in box rules at their factory settings so that your messages will stay in the in box rather than being filed automatically before you open them. As you open a message and read it, you can choose to act on it then and there.

After you've handled the message by replying or forwarding, you'll want to file it. For the greatest control over filing, touch the file button on the right side of the screen, as shown in Figure 8-4. The *File* window has buttons that let you file a *copy* of the message or *move* the message itself somewhere. By the way, this is the same *File* window that appears when you tap the *file* button in the lamp; the in box gives you this more convenient *file* button because filing is such a common operation in the in box.

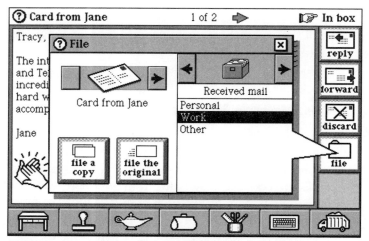

FIGURE 8-4. Filing a message that's in the in box

You can pick where you want to file the message by using a choice box that has the names of the file cabinet drawers and their folders. The choice box also offers to let you file the card in packages in main memory or on a memory card if one is installed in your communicator.

By using *file*, you can read through your customers' queries in whatever order you want, and then act on each one after you've read it and file it for future reference. If you use *file the original*, the message will vanish from your in box as it's filed away. By using *file a copy*, you can keep the message in your in box while you make a copy and file it.

If you're looking at the in box index, you can quickly file all the messages you see anywhere you choose, such as in a file cabinet folder or on a memory card package. To do this, tap the lamp to open it, and then tap the *file* button inside. You'll get the usual *File* window, except that the left side of the window, which tells you what you're filing, will indicate that you're about to file everything in the in box.

> **⚗ Humanizing the Interface.** Filing the contents of the in box demonstrates how hard Magic Cap tries to be human and friendly. If there's only one item in the in box, the *File* window tells you the name of the message's sender. If there are three or more items, the window says how many there are, as in *All 5 messages*. The most conversational message appears when there are two items; in that case, the window says that it's about to file *Both messages*.

There's another manual way to file messages in the file cabinet. You can slide a message from the in box index to the tote bag, open the appropriate drawer in the file cabinet, and then slide the message out of the tote bag and into a folder. This is great for beginners who aren't comfortable with the *file* button or for filing messages that you may have left sitting around on the desk or somewhere else. Don't be sloppy!

A Filing System for Incoming Mail

As you've probably noticed by now, Magic Cap tries hard to be adaptable to several different ways of working. In keeping with that theme, you can use yet another way to file your mail. This technique lets you read your messages in the in box, and then file them automatically according to specifications that you've set up.

There are two steps involved in using this technique. First, you'll make the folders you want and teach those folders what kind of messages they should attract. Then, you can use the *file all* button on the right side of the in box index, just below the button for collecting mail. When you tap *file all*, you'll be taken back to your desk, a folder will pop out of the file cabinet, and your messages will hop into the folders you set up.

Let's work through an example that uses this kind of filing. As a customer service representative for an office equipment retail store, you'll start by opening the drawer for *Received mail* and creating four folders, one for each line of products you support: copiers, fax machines, personal computers, and printers.

When you open a folder, the only button you'll see on the right side is labeled *sorting* (look back at Figure 8-3 to see this button when the folder is open). This is the button you'll use to tell the folder what kind of messages it should file. When you touch *sorting*, you'll see the *Sorting criteria* window (see Figure 8-5), which lets you set all kinds of instructions about what should be filed in this folder. The window has check boxes to turn each criterion on or off, as well as the appropriate choice boxes and text fields for typing.

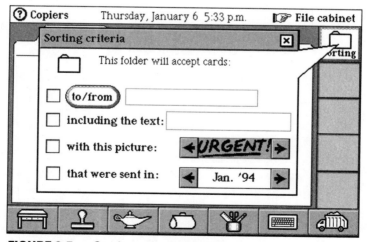

FIGURE 8-5. *Sorting criteria* window

You want to set up your new folders to hold messages about each of the four product lines. Tap the *Copiers* folder to open it, then tap *sorting* to set the criteria. You want this folder to hold any messages about copiers, so tap the check box that looks for particular words in the message, and then type *copier*.

You can repeat this process for each of your four folders. When you're done, the folders know how to accept the right messages. From now on, when you're looking at the in box index and you tap *file all*, any messages with the words you specified will automatically wind up in those folders without any further decisions by you. This shows how a little planning and preparation can go a long way!

If you want to set up a folder for messages from a specific customer, you can check the *to/from* box. When you do, the familiar name chooser will appear, and you can pick the name of the customer you want. When you get messages from that customer, tapping *file all* will put those messages in this folder.

Another sorting choice lets you file messages according to stamps that appear on them. You set this criterion with the choice box labeled *with this picture*. You can see the stamps by using the scroll arrows, or you can choose them by name from a list by touching the center of the choice box, as shown in Figure 8-6. Once you pick a stamp, messages with that stamp will be filed in this folder.

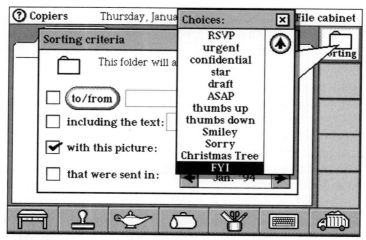

FIGURE 8-6. Choose a stamp by name

You can use the file-by-stamp feature to organize your incoming messages by stamping them yourself. For example, you might want to have a folder for mail you've received about new product procedures. After you read one of these messages, you can add an FYI stamp, even though the sender of the message didn't put that stamp on it. Then, when you touch *file all*, the FYI-stamped messages will jump into the folder you set up to accept messages with that stamp.

The final sorting criterion is the month and year the message was sent. You can use the check box's arrows to move forward and backward in time to pick the month you want. After you set this criterion, messages that were sent in the indicated month will be attracted to that folder when you *file all*.

What happens if you turn on more than one check box for a folder? The folder criteria work like this. If any of them is true for a message that you file, the message goes into that folder. For example, if you set up a folder to accept messages with the RSVP stamp or with the text *your party*, any messages with either that stamp or that text (or both) will wind up in the folder.

You can customize the set of stamps that's used for folder criteria. In the file cabinet scene, tap *stamps* to see the stamps that are available for folder criteria. You can add any new ones if you want, or you can remove stamps that you're sure you'll never use as filing criteria.

What if more than one folder wants a message? If you file a message that can match the criteria set up by more than one folder, the first folder in order in the drawer that wants it gets it. This lets you get really fancy and arrange your folders in a sort of hierarchy, with the most important ones getting first shot at messages.

If you haven't specified any rules when you tap *file all,* or if you have messages that don't respond to the criteria for any folders, your messages will be filed in a folder called *Other* in the *Received mail* drawer. Once they're there, you can move them into other folders whenever you want.

If you have stray messages sitting around, you can take advantage of the folder criteria you set up. Just slide these lost messages to the file cabinet on the desk. If the message was one you received, it'll go into the *Received mail* drawer; otherwise, it's filed in *Sent mail.* Inside the appropriate drawer, the message is filed according to the folder criteria you set up.

Filing Outgoing Mail

You can use the same folder criteria technique to file copies of your outgoing messages. For outgoing mail, the folder criteria work together with the out box rules. The out box rules let you file messages containing a specific word or certain stamps (urgent, confidential, or low priority), and they also let you choose to file into places other than the *Sent mail* drawer, such as another drawer or the tote bag. You can get filing options by setting the criteria for folders in the *Sent mail* drawer, but these out box rules and the folder criteria basically perform the same function.

One important note: To make sure that copies of all outgoing messages get filed, the out box rule *When any other message is sent, file it in the file cabinet* must be turned on (it's turned on at the factory). With this rule turned on, copies of all outgoing messages will wind up somewhere in the *Sent mail* drawer.

Let's say you want to order a jacket from Hendler's Emporium, a well-known store in downtown Magic Cap. You go downtown and pick out just the item you want to order. Hendler's has an electronic order form that you fill out and send directly to the store. You can order the purple suede jacket in size 10, and then mail the message to them. Because you have a folder set up for Hendler's in the *Sent mail* drawer of your file cabinet, you'll be able to keep a copy of your order, which includes the date and time stamped on the postmark.

Each time you send in an order, your copy of the order form is filed automatically in the folder. If your jacket isn't delivered in the promised two weeks, you have a copy of the order to refer to. If you hadn't set up a folder just for this store, a copy of the sent mail would have been filed in the *Other* folder in the *Sent mail* drawer.

Although the file folder criteria were created mainly for filing messages, they actually work for other items that you can file, including name cards and notebook pages. If you slide name cards or notebook pages to the file cabinet on the desk, they'll be filed in the *Sent mail* drawer according to the folders' criteria there.

The file cabinet has just one rule—how long to keep the items filed before trashing them. The rule is factory-set to throw out items after one month, but you can change the time setting. If you never want to throw anything away, you can turn the rule off completely. After all, who knows when you might need some note you wrote and sent four years ago?

Keeping things forever would be nice, but your communicator has limited memory, so you'll probably want to let the file cabinet throw things away after some time has elapsed. For those essential items that you want to be sure to keep around forever, you can mark with a Save stamp. Items marked that way will never get tossed by the file cabinet, even if their time has come.

Storeroom

Magic Cap includes a software version of extra closet space. It's called the storeroom, and you can find it by going down the hall, third door on your left. As you might expect from its name, the storeroom is the place where you manage the memory and items in your communicator. You can work with the communicator's main memory, any memory cards that are inserted, or a personal computer that's connected.

When you touch the storeroom door, it opens to reveal a directory, a personal computer set up on a table, and a shelving unit filled with boxes, some open and some closed, as you can see in Figure 8-7. The boxes on the shelves represent software packages, which are collections of objects that work inside your communicator.

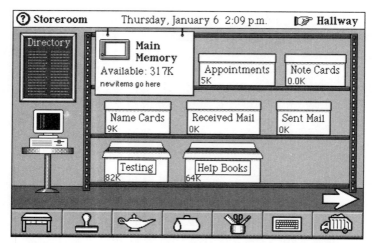

FIGURE 8-7. The storeroom shows software packages on shelves

The sign hanging in front of the shelves tells you what those shelves represent: main memory, a memory card, or a personal computer cabled to your communicator. You'll also see that each package is labeled with its contents and size.

There is a package for appointments, which, as you might guess, contains the contents of your datebook. Any package can be opened by touching it, and it hops off the shelf and opens to tell you what's inside. Like the hallway and downtown, the storeroom is wide enough to take up more than one screenful of information. You can tap the arrow on the floor to see more shelves off to the right, one for each memory card in the communicator.

The main memory shelves contain packages that represent important sets of information inside the communicator: appointments, note cards (pages in the notebook), name cards, received mail, and sent mail. When you touch a package, it jumps off the shelf, zooms open, and tells you a little bit about itself. Figure 8-8 is an example, showing you the inside of the appointments package.

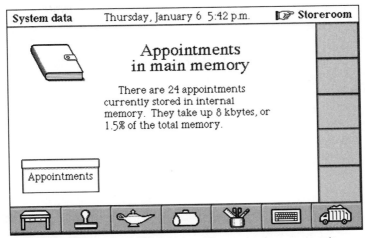

FIGURE 8-8. Information about the appointments package

🔮 **Please Touch.** Magic Cap users get used to the idea that they can touch items to make something happen. To support this, Magic Cap's designers tried to be sure that something happens (and something predictable) when you touch familiar items. As an example, the datebook that appears inside the appointments package isn't just an image, but the actual working model. If you touch this datebook, which is inside a box in the storeroom down the hall from your desk, it opens your datebook just as if you had gone back to the desk and touched the datebook there.

The bottom main memory shelf has an open package called *Help Books*. This package has the set of library books that came from the factory: *Getting Started*, *Secrets*, *Basics*, and others. This package looks open to show that it's *unpacked*, that is, its contents are visible and available for use. Magic Cap encourages you to support your local library, so you can check the books out at the library, which is just down the hall.

You might notice that the image for the *Help Books* package is different from the others. That's because the *Appointments*, *Note Cards*, *Name Cards*, *Received Mail*, and *Sent Mail* are special—they're system packages that always represent their specific kind of information inside the communicator. The *Help Books* and any packages you buy from software companies appear as boxes that can be open (unpacked and ready for use) or closed (packed up). You can pack up a package to make its contents unavailable, which will free some memory in the communicator, and then unpack it later when you need it. You can also get rid of it completely by sliding it to the trash, which will free a lot of memory, but you won't have the package any more.

Opening Packages

We looked at the inside of the appointments system package; now we'll open a standard package. Touch the *Help Books* package to open it (see Figure 8-9). This one tells who made it and when, and also provides some buttons along the right side. The first button, *pack up*, closes the package and puts its contents away, as discussed earlier. After you pack up the package, the button turns into an *unpack* command.

Help Books
version 1.0

pack up

go to

guide

Publisher: General Magic
Author: General Magic
Date Created: 1/10/94 6:13:41 a.m.
Last Modified: 1/6/95 2:11:48 p.m.
Size of Changes: 2584

Help Books

FIGURE 8-9.   Inside the Help Books package

Every package installs its items in the appropriate place in the Magic Cap world. Books are shelved in the library, games go in the game room, stationery forms go into the stationery drawer in the desk, and there are dozens of other places that can hold items from packages. You can tap *go to* if you want to be transported to the scene that holds the package's contents; for example, tapping *go to* from the *Help Books* takes you to the library.

Many packages come with some kind of built-in documentation. You can tap *guide* to see the documentation for these packages. The people who provide your software packages are interested in hearing from you, and because this is a communicator, it's easy to get in touch with them. Many packages include a *respond* button that creates a new message addressed to the package's publisher, giving you an easy way of registering for upgrades or complaining about something.

Memory Cards

Every Magic Cap communicator lets you store packages on memory cards, which are credit card–size storage devices that you can use to increase the amount of stuff your communicator can work with. They're known technically as PCMCIA cards, an acronym only a computer could love.

When you insert a memory card, a new shelving unit appears to represent it. A sign hangs in front of the shelves with the card's name, as pictured in Figure 8-10. You can use the shelves to move packages from main memory to the memory card, just like moving unused items into a trunk in the attic. You can use this feature to archive old appointments or little-used name cards by sliding the appropriate box to the memory card.

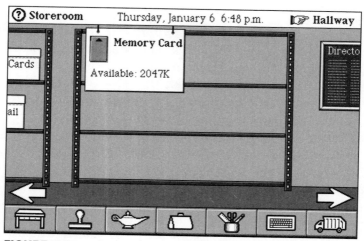

FIGURE 8-10.   Shelves for memory card

Items on the memory card are very much alive and accessible. When you insert a memory card, you can unpack its packages, which installs the packages' contents in their proper places. So, if you have a memory card with special name cards or old appointments, they'll appear in the name file or datebook when you insert the card.

Extending Main Memory with a Memory Card

You can extend your communicator's main memory by setting up a memory card as the place where all new items go. Here's a scenario: As an architect, you use the notebook frequently for sketches, and you may have to keep them for quite a while. It might be easiest to set up a memory card for your notebook, so every time you add another page, it automatically saves onto the memory card.

To do this, tap the memory card's sign. It zooms open to let you change its name or check the *new items* box. Tap the check box to turn it on, and then close the window. The sign now says *new items go here*, and whenever you make a new page in the notebook, everything will work as it usually does, except that the new page will be stored on the memory card.

When you have a memory card that's getting all the new items, it will also store any new name cards or appointments that you make. As long as the memory card is inserted, these items will act just as they would if they were in main memory—notebook pages appear in the notebook, appointments show up in the datebook, and so on. But as soon as you remove the card, anything that's stored on it will vanish.

To help you remember what's on the memory card, a tiny image of a memory card appears at the top left part of the screen for any item that's stored there. Figure 8-11 shows a notebook page from a memory card as an example. If you decide that the item is too important to keep on a memory card, you can tap the tiny memory card and Magic Cap will copy the item into main memory.

FIGURE 8-11. Tiny image at top shows important notebook page is on memory card

The storeroom has a few other details to keep you up to date on what's happening inside your communicator. There's a directory on the wall that lists the shelves you have. You'll also see a sign at the far right that shows you how much of your communicator's main memory is being used.

Backing Up and Connecting to a Personal Computer

The storeroom includes buttons in the lamp for backing up all your information to a memory card. Open the lamp, and then tap *back up* to save all your precious data. Then, if disaster strikes, you can insert the memory card that has your backup, and then tap *restore* in the lamp—it will all come back to you.

When you add an optional software package and cable, Magic Cap can connect to a personal computer. With this software installed on your personal computer, you can tap the computer in the storeroom to connect. Once you're connected, you can use the linked computer to back up your packages or as a source for installing new packages. You can also print using a printer connected to the computer.

Summary

The Magic Cap file cabinet was designed to behave just like file drawers in the physical world. There are standard drawers for *Sent mail* and *Received mail*, but you can make new drawers at the touch of a button. There are folders in each drawer that you can easily name. You can move folders around inside each drawer, and you can also move a folder with its contents to another drawer. You can file items manually by sliding them into the tote bag and then back out into a specified folder, or you can use the *file* command available in the lamp. There are also rules for filing in both the in box and out box scenes.

Each folder can be set with a variety of sorting criteria, which enables it to collect messages automatically. You can have incoming messages filed before you've read them based on who sent them, or on a certain word or stamp included in the message. You can file your mail according to when it was sent. You can also file the messages individually from the in box after you've read them.

The same sorting criteria can be used to file mail you've sent, too. Even if you don't specifically set a folder for mail, if you keep the factory-set rule turned on for filing all outgoing messages, copies of them will wind up in your file cabinet in a folder called *Other*. All folders tell the number of items inside them by showing a small number next to the name.

The main storage space in Magic Cap is the storeroom. It is set up with shelves containing packages that represent important items in your communicator. Each package is an active representative of its contents; you can open the *Appointments* package in the storeroom and see information about the appointments in your datebook. You can insert memory cards, which make new shelves for packages, to store information. Memory cards can also be used to extend your communicator's main memory. You can insert one and set it to store all newly created items so that as long as it's there, your communicator has that much more memory. As soon as you remove the card, though, that information is no longer accessible.

The storeroom scene also includes buttons in the lamp to back up your communicator's information to a memory card, or even to a personal computer if you have additional accessories.

Chapter 9

 Other Features

Details and Loose Ends

When I'm working, there are lots of little things that I need that aren't directly part of the work I'm doing. Supplies and tools, like a dictionary and thesaurus, are essential, plus some sticky notes and a pen. The environment is important, like having music to fill the background and having a glass of water or can of cream soda. And a stapler. And maybe some paper clips, and the three-hole punch. And my calendar. And the clock. And...well, you get the idea.

I may not need to use all those things on any particular day, but if I do, I don't want to interrupt my work to go dig them up someplace. I like to have easy access to the things I might need right where I need them, even if I never do need them. There are lots of these kinds of accessories designed into Magic Cap. There are also storage spaces that stay empty until some farsighted software developer creates a package to fill a need, like an accounting package to live in your desk drawer or games for the game room, or a whole travel agency downtown.

Some of these details are vital, like the control panels and the library. There are others that you might never use, such as the calculator. You might never notice the clock after setting it once because it just blends into the Magic Cap world. Depending on your interests, it's possible that you could walk right past the game room in the hallway without bothering to peek inside. Magic Cap's designers worked to make sure that these extra features wait patiently until you need them.

Time and Date

A clock is typically an indispensable feature in almost any environment. Hanging prominently on the wall behind your desk, the clock is a nice analog one that not only shows the current time, but it also has controls to set the time and date and even to show you different time zones.

As you might guess, you can set the clock by touching it. When you touch the clock, it zooms up close to show you a calendar, a bigger analog clock with a digital time display below it, and four buttons on the right edge to show you other parts of the clock (see Figure 9-1). The top button, *display*, is already highlighted to tell you that this scene simply displays the current time and today's date. This scene is strictly for looking; to set the clock, you touch *set time*, and to change the date, you use *set date*.

✎ **Up to date.** For years, computer engineers have been putting the time and date together. After all, they know that the time and date are really the same thing mathematically—the time is just a way to talk about the date in finer detail. But Magic Cap's designers observed that most people think of the time and date as two separate things. To match this expectation, Magic Cap always explicitly refers to the time and date separately, as in the *Getting Started* lesson named *Set the time and date*.

Touch *set time* when you want to change the time of the clock inside your communicator. It will look like the scene in Figure 9-2.

FIGURE 9-1. Clock scene shows date and time

FIGURE 9-2. Set the time and indicate your time zone

The left side of the scene shows an analog clock. You can just slide the hands of the clock to set the time. A digital display above the analog clock has arrows that let you change the hours and minutes with more precision. The right side of the scene has a button at the top that lets you tell Magic Cap what time zone you're in by picking a city in your time zone. If you tap this button, you'll see a list of prominent international cities. Pick your city, or if the city you're in isn't listed, choose one that's in your time zone. You may have to settle for another city in your time zone instead of your exact location (sorry, Seattle).

Two check boxes on the right side of the scene complete your time-keeping options. If your city is observing Daylight Savings Time right now, tap the check box to set it. There's a check box you can use to always display 24-hour time in digital clocks and in text if that's how you want it. When you're done, tap *accept,* and the new time is set and the scene switches back to the clock display. In practice, you'll really have no need to set the time unless your communicator is brand new or all your batteries died and you need to start over again. However, when you travel, you can use the *set time* feature to choose the time zone you're in and the clock will change accordingly.

The *set date* button displays the calendar for the month, with today's date highlighted, as shown in Figure 9-3. This calendar looks just like the ones in other parts of Magic Cap, with arrows at the top to set the month and arrows at the bottom to change the year. To set the date, just use the arrows to pick the right month and year, then touch today's date on the calendar. Magic Cap knows about the international date line, so setting your new time zone when you travel will also take care of changing the date, if necessary. Unless you have fatal battery problems or a time machine, you won't need to reset the date.

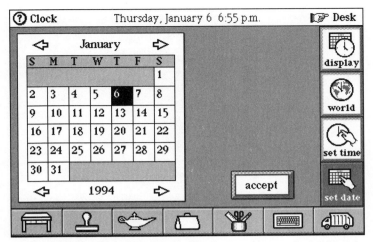

FIGURE 9-3. Setting today's date

The fourth button in this scene is the intriguing *world*, and if you look very closely at Figure 9-1, you'll see that the button has a picture of clock hands on a globe. This button shows you Magic Cap's world clock, which lets you answer that age-old question, "If it's 3:10 P.M. in Iowa, what time is it in Tokyo?" (Give yourself 25 bonus points if you knew that the answer is 6:10 A.M. the following day.)

The world clock, pictured in Figure 9-4, shows a map of the world with time zones drawn in, along with panels showing the time and day in four cities. The cities are also highlighted by points on the map itself. The world clock lets you see what time it is in four different places at once.

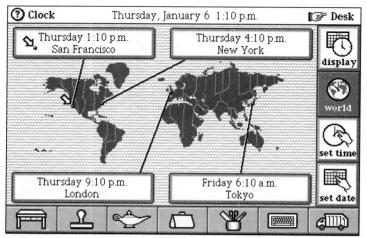

FIGURE 9-4. World clock shows the time in four cities

If you're not fond of the cities shown in the world clock, you can change them. Touch any of the time panels to select a different city from Magic Cap's list. It's the same list that you saw when choosing your time zone in the *set time* screen. (This is one of the few lists in Magic Cap that doesn't allow you to add your own entries.)

The map includes a funky arrow pointing to the city you chose for your time zone, kind of like those maps at the mall with a reassuring "you are here." If you set a panel to show a different city, the time in that panel changes to reflect the new city you chose. You can also select a city by holding down the option key while you touch a point on the map. The city nearest your touch goes into one of the panels.

Once you've selected a new city from the list, there's a check box you should set if that city is observing daylight savings time. When you touch *accept*, the panel and time are changed to that new location. By the way, you're not going crazy if you thought you saw something swimming in the waves of the South Pacific.

Desk Drawers and the Calculator

The desk includes two drawers for keeping important items you may need. The left drawer holds your stationery, easy enough to get to, but stashed away out of sight until you need it. The drawer on the right has room for miscellaneous desk accessories, including the calculator that comes with every Magic Cap communicator. The calculator is the only standard item that Magic Cap puts in the desk accessories drawer, but you might imagine this drawer also holding maps of major cities or sets of income tax forms.

The calculator, like other Magic Cap tools, gives you choices about how it can best meet your needs. Figure 9-5 shows you what the calculator looks like. With the choice box set to *Paper Tape*, the calculator prints all its work on a built-in paper tape. You can see your calculations as you enter them, which is great if there are a lot of numbers, as the tape holds 100 lines of information.

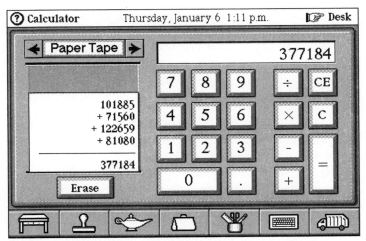

FIGURE 9-5. Magic Cap's calculator has a paper tape

If you hold down the option key, you can tear the results off the tape as a text coupon and put them in the tote bag. If you need to attach the calculations to a message to your boss about project expenses, you could create the new message and then slide the tape out of the tote bag to your message.

When you slide the coupon out of the tote bag, it automatically reproduces all the text from the tape, so your boss can see exactly how you calculated the expenses. You could also slide the paper tape out of the tote bag and onto your notes that are attached to the budget meeting scheduled in your datebook. You might also use the numbers when you slide them out of the tote bag onto a blank notebook page to include in your presentation at the budget meeting. You get the idea.

Copycat.   You might remember that Magic Cap often uses option-slide to copy things, such as items in the tote bag, pages in the notebook index, or addresses on a name card. It works here, too; option-slide moves a copy of your calculations from the paper tape in the calculator. If you're going to use the same calculations in other places, option-slide the coupon out of the tote bag to move a copy of the tape. The original paper tape remains in the calculator until you press the button to erase it.

If you don't need the paper tape, you can set the calculator to Basic, which replaces the paper tape with several buttons. One particularly useful button on the basic calculator helps you figure tips. You'll find a place to set the tip percentage. Touch the plus sign to move up from 15% if you're a big tipper, or the minus sign if the service wasn't great. When the lunch bill comes, you can enter the total bill, adjust the percentage, and then hit the *tip* button to quickly calculate the tip. Of course, you won't need this if there's someone at your table who can figure percentages in his or her head, which happens often in Silicon Valley where I live.

The third choice for the calculator is *Scientific*, which provides keys that engineers and scientists would expect to find on a scientific calculator, hence the descriptive name. For people who understand why there's a switch to choose between radians and degrees, along with buttons for arc, sine, cosine, and tangent, no further explanation is necessary about the power of the scientific calculator. For the rest of us who don't understand those things, no further explanation is necessary, either.

The Hallway and Controls

When you're not working at the desk in your communicator, you'll use the hallway as the corridor to get you between your desk and other interesting places, including downtown. The hallway includes several useful places behind its doors, as well as some whimsy. Magic Cap's designers obviously remember what was said about all work and no play.

When you're at the desk, you can get to the hallway by touching the step-back hand in the upper-right corner of the screen (see Figure 9-6). The directory on the wall opens with a touch. The directory isn't just a map of the rooms in your hallway—you can touch anything in the list, and you'll zip down the hall and watch the door open for you. You can get there in more leisurely fashion by touching the arrows on the floor and tapping the door yourself.

Directory

Desk

Library

Contr

FIGURE 9-6. The hallway shows how to get to other rooms

Going through the hallway's first door takes you to back to your desk; of course, you can always touch the desk button at the lower-left corner of the screen to get to the desk. Touch the step-back hand while in the hallway to go directly downtown. Touch the arrow on the floor to move farther along down the hall so you can get to more rooms.

Along with the doors, there's a panel on the wall that leads to Magic Cap's controls. The control panel is the place where you can set preferences for the way your communicator behaves in certain situations. Inside the control panel are buttons that open scenes containing settings for different parts of your communicator, as you can see in Figure 9-7. You can also hold down the option key and touch the lamp from any scene in Magic Cap as a shortcut to the control panel. The control panel includes buttons for several sets of controls, including *general*, *screen*, *sound*, *power*, *privacy*, and *signature*.

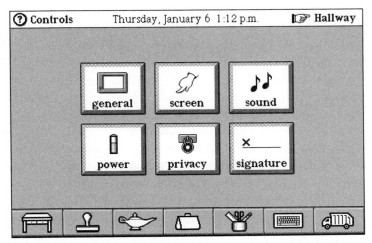

FIGURE 9-7. Buttons that lead to various control panels

The *general* panel includes settings to display items at the top of the screen in every scene. There's a check box to display the battery level of your communicator. You'll also find check boxes for displaying today's date and the current time at the top of the screen.

In addition to the three check boxes that let you show things at the top of the screen, there are three more check boxes for miscellaneous options. You can have your communicator ask for confirmation before you do permanent or destructive things, such as discarding a name card or setting the current user. If you are pretty sure about your Magic Cap expertise, you might turn off the warnings and take your chances. Of course, even if you fail to heed the warnings, you can usually pull recently discarded items from the trash.

Another check box lets you hear the phone dialing when you make a call. If you like to hear the number being dialed and the modems screaming at each other while the connection is being made, you can keep this option on. The third option you can set in the general control panel is whether construction mode is turned on or off. With construction mode turned on, you have access to warehouses full of fun stuff in the magic hat, and you get the tinker tool for going behind the scenes and changing the behavior of items. For lots more in-depth information on Magic Cap's version of home improvement, you can peek ahead to Chapter 10.

The *screen* button only lets you adjust one thing—your touch screen. When you use this control panel, you'll repeat the initial screen setup that asks you to touch a target that hops around the screen. Use this control panel if your communicator seems to be feeling your touches in the wrong place.

Magic Cap uses sound effects as an integral part of the user interface; the sound effects were designed to make you feel more confident about the actions you're taking. These sound effects, along with the ability to play digitized songs, are why there's a control panel dedicated to sound. Some talented music-meisters worked on Magic Cap's sounds, including musician/composer/producer/interactive artist Todd Rundgren.

When you touch the *sound* button, which is decorated by musical notes, you see a screenful of sound effects along with the names of the actions that play the sounds. For example, there are sounds for a door opening and closing, a window going away, or a switch flipping. You can put other sounds here to change what you hear when you use Magic Cap. There's also a sliding volume control that goes from silent to almost obnoxious.

The *power* control panel gives you a graphic display of how much juice is left in your main and backup batteries, which is why there's an image of a battery on the button. This is also where you instruct your communicator how long to wait before shutting off to save power. There's a check box that lets you decide whether the communicator should automatically shut off even if it's plugged in. Keeping this check box turned on will speed up the battery recharging time on some communicators.

The *privacy* button is aptly represented by a padlock. This control panel lets you set a security password for your communicator. You get to decide whether you need to protect your information from a nosy co-worker or a fearless eight-year-old. If you decide to go for it, there's a button to set your secret password on a telephone-style keypad. There's also a choice box that lets you designate how often you want your communicator to check security. You can instruct it to ask for a password every time it turns on, once an hour, once a day, or never.

The final control panel, *signature*, is certainly the most personal. This button takes you to a scene that lets you add your signature to Magic Cap (see Figure 9-8). Arrows point out the signature lines, one for just your first name and one for your full name, and you also see a smaller box that shows you a reduced view of your signature. Each line has an erase button so you can keep trying until you get it the way you want. After you sign your name, you'll find stamps available in the stamper with your personal signatures, available for your use on messages or anywhere else.

The control panel is always just a few steps away from your desk, and there will be times when you'll need to change a setting. Most of the time, the control panel will be the kind of place that's nice to visit, but you wouldn't want to have to live there.

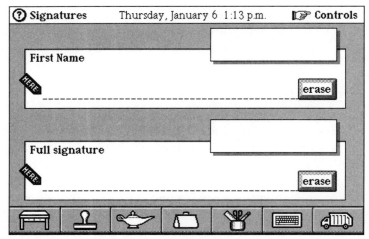

FIGURE 9-8. Adding your signatures

Library

Some futurists claim that computers and interactive materials will render printed books virtually obsolete. On the other side of the argument, traditionalists say that the powerful experience of reading a book can't easily be replaced by new technology. Magic Cap tries to balance these two views with the library, which you can visit by going down the hallway (see Figure 9-9).

The library is filled with books that really look and act like the books you're used to; it even has a card catalog that maintains an inventory of the books there. Of course, these are electronic replicas of books, with no paper to tear and no jackets to lose, only information-filled pages. Magic Cap takes advantage of the fact that books provide a familiar way to browse information by having tips for using your communicator written in volumes you can read in the library.

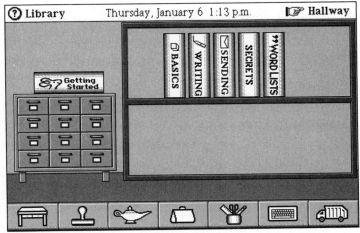

FIGURE 9-9. Your own personal library has room for many books

Back in Chapter 1 we looked at the *Getting Started* lessons that help you navigate through Magic Cap's setup procedures. You can find all those lessons in the *Getting Started* book in the library. When you open that volume, you see book pages that are not only literately written for a beginning user, but also buttons on each page that take you to the necessary place in Magic Cap and step you through each action to set up and teach you about your communicator.

Synchronicity. If you're more savvy and you prefer to skip the lessons and set things up yourself, the Getting Started book knows how to update itself when you complete an action. For example, if you bypass the lessons and figure out that you can personalize your communicator by making a new name card for yourself, the corresponding page in *Getting Started* now tells you that your name card has already been set up, and it removes the step-by-step lesson button.

Touching the folded-down corner at the top of a page turns to the next or previous page of the book, and you shortcut fans can hold down option while touching the corner to move to the book's first or last page. Even if you passed all the *Getting Started* lessons when you first started using your communicator, the book stays on the library shelf for future reference in case you need a refresher course.

Books

Getting Started is not the only important reference in your library. There's a book called *Basics* that goes over some of the general features of Magic Cap. *Basics* provides a thorough introduction to your communicator's features, working together with the user manual to help you get the most out of your communicator (and depending on which model of communicator you have, the user manual and *Basics* may even have been written by the same person).

Each time you open a book in the library, there are three buttons that appear on the right side of the screen, as you can see in the *Basics* screen shown in Figure 9-10. The first one is *shelve*, which puts the book away for you when you're done. The second button, *contents*, turns the pages to show you the table of contents. As you might expect, the contents page doesn't just show you what topics are in the book—it actually helps you get to them. When you touch a chapter name or page number on the contents page, the book flips directly to the page you want.

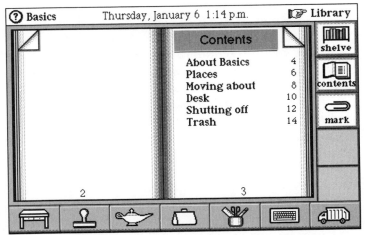

Contents

About Basics	4
Places	6
Moving about	8
Desk	10
Shutting off	12
Trash	14

shelve

contents

mark

2   3

FIGURE 9-10. *Basics* book and its buttons on the right

The *mark* button, the third one down on the right, shows an image of a paper clip, and that tells you what it does: It clips a page for quick reference. It's similar to the physical world's neon yellow highlight pen, marking a page with a tiny paper clip on the page's entry in the table of contents and on the page itself. Unlike the yellow highlight marks, the paper clip mark is easily removed by touching the button again; it changes to *unmark* if the page is already marked. Also, these marks don't have that funny marker smell.

The library also includes a book that contains helpful tips on creating and editing messages. There's another book that includes some generic instructions on sending messages. *Secrets* is a fun book that contains a few examples of the "power user" features of Magic Cap. You don't need to know any of these tricks or shortcuts to effectively and efficiently use your communicator, but they're in there if you want to read about them.

Word Lists

The other standard reference in your library is *Word Lists*. This volume contains all the words your communicator uses for the automatic word-completion feature we saw in Chapter 5. For example, this is where you'll find the list of first names that Magic Cap can guess from to save you typing when you're entering a name card. There are lists of cities, states, and countries that are also used for auto-completing words.

The word lists can be built automatically or manually. You'll typically add words automatically: When you add new information to name cards, the words are added to the proper word list. Because you entered your name card, your last name was added to the Last Names word list. When you enter a name card for a family member with the same last name, the automatic completion feature will guess at the last name because you already taught it yours, as you may remember from our examples about Susan and Mark Anthony and their friend Hans Anderson in Chapter 5.

Every time you add a name card, the entry you type for first name, last name, company name, job title, city, state, and country will be added to the appropriate word list if it's not already there. This is how Magic Cap can remember a long name, like the law firm of Jacksons, Monk, and Rowe, so you only have to type it in once even though you'll enter several name cards for contacts you have there. Magic Cap communicators really do learn from you, and you don't have to teach them the lessons over and over again.

You can also add new words manually by opening the *Word Lists* book and touching the *add* button that each chapter includes. There's also a *change* button to correct spelling mistakes and a *remove* button to reclaim memory by getting rid of entries that you won't use.

Let's say you're a doctor and you need to use your communicator to jot down some notes about a patient when you're at home. Let's also say that you don't have the best handwriting, so you might want to type the note. Typing is tough on a communicator's small on-screen keyboard.

One of the tricks Magic Cap uses to reduce typing is a system for automatically expanding abbreviations. You can add abbreviations that you use often to the word lists, and then after you've typed them, you can expand them by touching the keyboard's *expand* key after typing the abbreviation. If you have to write notes about hospital patients, you might want to add an abbreviation to the word list. Adding abbreviations is straightforward: turn to the *Abbreviations* page, touch *add*, and then type in the abbreviation followed by the words it represents.

You might enter MMC to stand for Mercy Medical Center. Then, whether you're adding a name card for someone at the hospital or sending a message to another doctor who will be seeing your patients today, you can type *mmc* (upper- or lowercase are treated the same way), then touch *expand*, and you've cut your keystrokes from 20 to 4. You can enter as many abbreviations as you want to minimize your typing and take maximum advantage of your communicator.

Play, Art, and Work

As you go down the hallway, you probably noticed the *Game room* door with a playing card on it. This room was added to give you a break once in a while and provide a place for you to keep games. When you open the game room door, you'll see shelves with space for games and other fun packages. There's also one of those cool cat clocks on the wall that has the cat's swinging tail as the pendulum, a subtle reminder of how much time is passing while you're playing games.

Magic Cap has a coin in the game room that you can flip by touching. Heads is the General Magic bunny in his hat, and tails is the rabbit's rear end. You can look forward to games from third-party developers to fill the shelves of the game room, and it'll be especially cool to see interactive games that use beaming or other kinds of communication so several people can play. Until then, the game room's coin will be handy when you have to choose where to go for lunch.

There are a couple of other things you will see in the hallway that aren't really essential, but they are appealing and fun (see Figure 9-11). There's a painting hanging on the wall. By touching the painting, you can switch between images, from Picasso to Matisse and back to Picasso. If you hold down the option key and touch the painting, you can have the name of the artist displayed below the painting for your less-cultured associates.

You can even have the picture change automatically every day, or add your own images to the rotation. While Magic Cap includes just these two masterpieces, a savvy developer could produce collections of image art for you to hang on your wall, courtesy of a memory card or an image gallery downtown.

Near the end of the hallway is a plaque that displays the General Magic logo. When you touch the plaque, you'll see a list of all the dedicated people who brought you Magic Cap and Telescript, plus some required copyright and legal stuff. You might not ever touch this sign, but you can remember that it's a credit to the people who are proud of their work and are thrilled to put their names on it.

FIGURE 9-11. The hallway has a painting and a credits plaque

Summary

Magic Cap tries very hard to simulate a comfortable working environment. Many of the tools you'll use often are placed in, on, and around your desk. You can walk down the hallway to find other useful places, including rooms, control panels, and tables with drawers that open. You can stroll downtown, visiting stores that offer merchandise and services.

All of these places and lots of others have been designed to accept additional packages and services from third-party developers. For example, you might buy a package of stamps with licensed logos of Major League Baseball teams. When you install the package, it will automatically add another drawer to the stamper. You might buy a memory card with a check-writing package that knows how to move into your desk drawer when you unpack it, or you might receive an electronic signup form for a news information service that builds a building downtown that you can visit to request new topics.

Every Magic Cap communicator includes a clock and a calendar. You'll set them once when you first set up your communicator, and you can reset them if you ever need to. The clock also includes a scene that shows the time in four international cities of your choice.

You can use the calculator in the desk drawer to perform simple computations, put numbers on a tape that you can move into a message or elsewhere, or handle scientific calculations.

The hallway has control panels that let you set preferences for how your communicator works. There are settings that let you display the date, time, and battery strength at the top of the screen all the time. Other controls turn on construction mode, extra warnings, and phone-dialing sounds. The control panels also help you adjust the touch screen, choose sound effects, determine whether the communicator should shut off automatically when not in use, set a password, and sign your name.

Magic Cap has a library that holds books about how to use the communicator. Some books have special features, like built-in lessons or lists of words that affect typing. Software developers can add more books with all kinds of information.

For people who need a diversion close at hand, there's a game room with a flipping coin and space for other fun packages. Finally, the hallway includes a magic painting that changes its images and a plaque listing the names of the people who created Magic Cap and Telescript.

Chapter 10

/> Construction

Get Your Hard Hat

I like Magic Cap just the way it is. What's not to like? The desk looks fine, I like the colors and sounds, and the tools for drawing are OK with me. Magic Cap's designers worked hard to include everything they believed would be useful to the average communicator owner, maybe someone like me. However, the designers wanted Magic Cap to have the power of a higher level of customization. While most of us would be horrified at moving objects that aren't supposed to move, some people want to be able to redecorate their scenes. These people like adding their own sounds to buttons, or putting together their own check boxes and buttons.

For these tinkerers who want to customize Magic Cap using more than just stamps, there's construction mode. If you enjoy a little power-using once in a while, this chapter may be helpful for you, especially if you figure out how it can save you some time.

Construction Mode

You can start doing construction by flipping on the *construction mode* check box in the general control panel. Turning on construction mode affects what you see in every scene. The first thing you'll notice is that the stamper image on the bottom of the screen changes into an upside-down top hat, reminiscent of the hats used by magicians and their rabbits. When you tap the magic hat, a window opens to show you all the categories of stuff inside (see Figure 10-1).

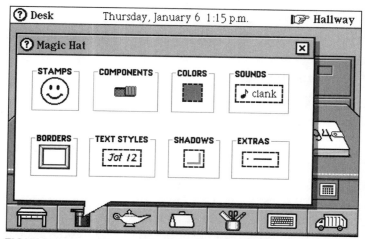

FIGURE 10-1. The magic hat shows its categories of items

When you tap a category's image, the screen changes to show you more of that category's contents. As you can see, stamps are just one category inside the hat; the happy face stamp represents the stamper and all its drawers, and they're still available just as they were without construction mode.

The second effect of construction mode is that you'll get access to more tools in every scene. For example, every scene gets to use the *move, copy,* and *stretch* tools, which are normally available only in certain scenes, such as the notebook, where you usually do lots of drawing.

When you're doing construction, you can use these tools with many more items, which is why they're available in every scene.

The third effect of construction mode is to add commands in the lamp. Various scenes will add their own commands to the lamp in construction mode; for example, because you can rearrange items on the desk in construction mode, you'll also get a *clean up* command for the desk. The only lamp command that's added for every scene is *snap*, which takes a magic snapshot of the current scene. You can move a snapshot elsewhere and use it to go back to the scene instantly, or slide things into the snapshot to send them to the scene it pictures.

In addition to producing the magic hat and adding tools and commands, scenes can be affected by construction mode in various custom ways. For example, when you're in construction mode the control panel adds dialing controls that let you set fine details like whether to speed up or slow down the dialing.

 Trying it Out. You can get a preview of construction mode without actually flipping the switch. When you open the stamper, hold down the option key while you touch the stamps window's title bar. The magic hat window replaces the stamps window and you see what's in Figure 10-1. The effect is only temporary; after you make a selection and close the window, and then tap the stamper again to open it, it will be just stamps again. If you're going to use more than one effect from the magic hat, you might as well turn on construction mode from the control panel.

Custom Forms

Let's say it's your turn to be in charge of ordering lunch for the departmental staff meeting. Twelve people in your department depend on their communicators because they're out on the road quite a bit, so you know that sending an electronic message is the fastest way to reach them. You also know, though, that just because you send the message doesn't mean they'll take the time to write a complete message in reply.

To make it easier on them and you, you create a message that includes choice boxes so they can select their preferences for lunch and then easily send the message back with those choices. Start by touching the postcard on the desk and addressing it to the group *The Department*, which you created earlier. You type the message confirming the date, time, and location of the meeting, and then you ask them to respond with their choices for lunch.

Now for the fun part. With construction mode turned on, touch the magic hat to open it. In the magic hat, touch *components* to see the parts inside. The drawers are like those in the stamper; you want to open the one labeled *choices*. You touch it and see the page of choice boxes, meters, and sliding controls, as shown in Figure 10-2. Touch the choice box; by keeping your finger on it, you can stamp one out and slide it right into the position you want on the postcard.

If you option-touch the magic hat again, you get right back to the same drawer, where you can add two more choice boxes (this is a long meeting). Now you've got the message written and three choice boxes with meaningless choices. The next step is to make the choices mean something.

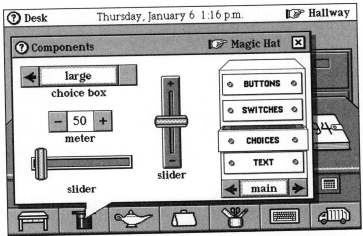

FIGURE 10-2. Choice boxes available in the magic hat

To start doing this, option-touch the keyboard to get to the label maker. Type *sandwich,* and then tear it off by sliding it over to the top choice box and dropping it right on the choice box's label. You'll hear the slurping sound that means the choice box has accepted the new coupon. The choice box is now called *sandwich.*

Go back to the label maker (option-touch the keyboard) to type the choices. Type these words and press *return* between each choice: *turkey, vegetarian, ham & Swiss.* Tear the coupon off, slide it over, and drop it right on the middle of the choice box. With a slurp, the choice box now has three new choices. Repeat the same steps for the middle choice box for salad and the bottom choice box for dessert. The result is shown in Figure 10-3.

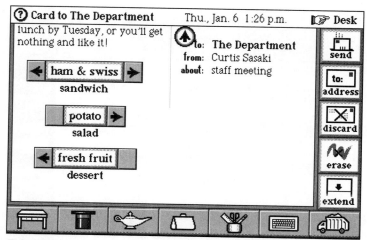

FIGURE 10-3. The message and its custom choice boxes

You've just custom-made three choice boxes that Magic Cap's designers couldn't possibly have programmed for you, and you did it with a minimum amount of work. Now you can send off the message and wait for replies. Each recipient can make choices on the message, and then touch *forward* to send it back to you. (Remember that forwarded messages have the original message attached.) Before the end of the day, you've received all 12 lunch orders for the staff meeting, and you didn't even have to leave your communicator's desk.

A Magic Invitation

The *components* drawers in the magic hat are full of lots of interesting things to play with besides choice boxes. In the *switches* drawer, you can use various switches and check boxes to make your messages more interactive. Let's try out a check box example.

Chapter 4 showed how you can get Magic Cap's datebook to automatically invite people to a meeting.

This time, we'll make a party invitation, and then use electronic mail to invite people manually. In this example, you want to throw a surprise birthday party for your spouse. Because it's a surprise, you have to avoid having people call your house with an RSVP. Here's a perfect way to use your communicator to not only send the invitations, but also get back the responses. Not all of your friends have Magic Cap communicators yet, so the check box won't work for everyone, but for the ones who do, responding to an invitation is a snap.

After you've designed the invitation, you can go to the magic hat *components* and choose a check box. By touching it and not letting up on your touch, you can slide it right onto the invitation. You option-touch the keyboard, type *I'll be there!* on the label maker, tear it off, and then slide it over and drop it on the check box to rename it. The invitation is ready to send off to your friends.

When your invitation is received, all the guest will have to do is touch the box to make the check mark, (or not change it at all if the answer is no) and then forward it back to you. The forwarded message has a copy of the original message attached, so when you receive the message back, you can see from the check box whether or not the sender can come. The party is more likely to stay a surprise because you are the only person receiving the replies.

Customizing Sounds and Images

We've seen the kinds of things you can do with items from the *components* drawers in the magic hat. Now, let's look at some of the other things construction mode can help you do.

Back in Chapter 7, we saw how a creative kid could make a birthday card with sound and animation. We stamped a cartoon onto a notebook page, then got another stamp that played a song, and dropped the song stamp onto the animation, in effect adding a soundtrack to the cartoon. In construction mode, we can expand on the idea of adding sound effects to actions.

One of the sounds heard most often in Magic Cap is the click that's made when you touch something to open it or tap a button along the bottom of the screen. You've decided you're getting a little bored with that sound and you want to take advantage of some of the other sounds Magic Cap plays. The magic hat has a set of drawers labeled *sounds* filled with sound coupons that you can drop anywhere to replace the factory-set sounds.

Touch the magic hat to open it, and then touch *sounds*. Inside is a drawer called *instruments*, which is where you decide to begin your customizing. You touch the *clarinet* stamp, and then slide it off onto the desk button in the lower-left corner. Every time you touch the desk button from now on, you'll hear a quick blast on the clarinet instead of the old click. Like a mad composer, you continue on across the screen: the stamper gets a piano note, the lamp plays like a guitar, the tote bag becomes a trumpet, the tool holder sounds like the string section of an orchestra, the keyboard gets the snare, and the trash truck sounds like a crashing cymbal when you throw something away. Talk about your *personal* communicator.

There are other items in the magic hat that affect images. The coupons for colors, borders, text styles, and shadows all change the way Magic Cap items look. You can use these tools to vary the text styles that the keyboard types, change the coloring or shadowing of an object, or choose different kinds of borders for the things that use them.

Magic Hat Extras

The final category in the magic hat is called *extras*, and it offers all the goodies that didn't fit anywhere else, which means it includes some of the highest-level customizing features in Magic Cap. When you touch *extras*, you'll see drawers that let you change tools in the tool holder. You can add various kinds of line styles or shape types to the tool holder just by touching the appropriate coupon and sliding it into the tote bag. Then, when you open the specific set of tools in the tool holder, slide the coupon into that window; it becomes a choice you can select the next time you're using the tools.

Another interesting drawer in *extras* is the one called *properties*. When you touch this drawer to open it, you'll see coupons that affect the way items appear on the screen (see Figure 10-4). You can choose coupons to hide items or show everything that's been hidden. There are coupons that layer objects by bringing them closer to the screen or sending them to the back. Two opposing coupons set an item so you can either throw it away or keep it from being thrown away. Other coupons rotate objects 90 degrees or flip them 180 degrees.

The *flip* and *rotate* coupons work on shapes. You could slide a *rotate* coupon into the tote bag, choose an arrow tool, and draw an arrow on a blank notebook page. As we saw in Chapter 7, you can draw an arrow pointing left or right, depending on which way you slide your finger as you're drawing it. You can now take the rotate coupon out of the tote bag, drop it onto your sideways arrow, and suddenly it points up or down. This could be useful the next time you draw a map.

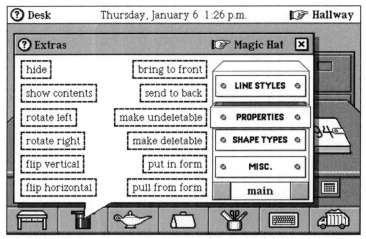

FIGURE 10-4. The *properties* drawer in magic hat *extras*

Tinkering

Now that you've seen some of the uses for construction mode, let's take a closer look at the ultimate construction item, the *tinker* tool. This tool, which looks like a wrench, appears in the *authoring* tool set along with *move*, *copy*, and *stretch*. With construction mode turned on, touch the tool holder, and then touch the wrench. It hops into the tool holder and becomes the active tool.

Tinkering lets you see inside objects and change things that otherwise wouldn't be changeable. When you touch an item with the wrench, you'll see a window that tells you something about that item in terms of coupons and settings. Let's go to the painting in the hallway and tinker with it. Your goal is to take it off the wall in the hallway and move it behind the desk so you can see it more often. This may take quite a few steps, but for a person who likes to tinker, getting there is most of the fun.

The first thing to do is choose the *move* tool and try sliding the painting into the tote bag. It doesn't work; the factory setting for the painting prevents you from moving it. Let's try tinkering with it to see what might be wrong. With construction mode turned on, touch the tool holder, go to the *authoring* tools, and then touch the wrench. It hops into the tool holder, becoming the active tool.

Now let's open up the painting and look behind the scenes. Touch the painting; instead of changing the art, as normally happens when you touch it, you see a window that shows some interesting stuff about the painting, as shown in Figure 10-5. There are coupons for the border and the sound; some controls for the painting's label; and check boxes that indicate whether it can be moved, copied, or stretched.

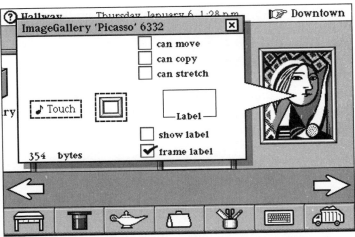

FIGURE 10-5. The painting's tinkering window tells all about it

This is pretty interesting: The *can move* check box is turned off. Could that be what's preventing us from moving the painting? Touch the *can move* box to check it, and then close the window. Go back to the tool holder to get the *move* tool and try sliding the painting into the tote bag. It works! Just like in a magic show, the whole painting fits comfortably in that little tote bag.

Now tap the desk button to go back to the desk. To make room for rehanging the painting on the wall behind the desk, you have to move the in box and the out box over a bit so they don't cover up the image. You get to tinker with two more things, using the *move* tool to move them one at a time.

When there's enough room on the wall, you can schlepp the painting out of the tote bag to its new home behind your desk. Uh, oh. It's too big, and it covers up half of your notebook. Let's try using a coupon from the magic hat's *extras* to send it to the back so it gets tucked in behind your desk. Open the magic hat, touch *extras,* and open the *properties* drawer. Touch *send to back,* slide it onto the painting, and—presto! The Picasso hangs behind your desk. If you touch it, it switches to the Matisse, just as when it was hanging in the hallway (see Figure 10-6). Looks like you could use a smaller desk, though.

In: 1   Out

'94

FIGURE 10-6.   The painting has been rehung behind the desk

Another Tinkering Project

As long as we're redecorating, let's change the image on the library door. You could try stamping a happy face on the door, but if you did, the stamp would just end up going inside the room. You need to get a coupon that has the image of the happy face stamp, and then replace the image on the door with your custom-selected image. Okay, tinkerers, start your wrenches.

The first thing you do is get the stamp that has the face image. As long as you're going to be changing the library door, you might as well just put it on the floor in the hallway (see Figure 10-7). Now, get the wrench from the tool holder, and then touch the stamp again to see its secrets. Slide the stamp's image coupon out of the window and onto the library door.

FIGURE 10-7. Tinkering with the happy face stamp

You'll hear the slurp sound, see the visual highlighting effect, and the next thing you know, your library door has a smiling face. Because you should always clean up when you're done, you can throw away the stamp you stole the image coupon from. You're now ready for your next real task, or even more tinkering, if you prefer.

You can look forward to bright third-party developers using tinkering and construction to whip up some impressive accessories and packages for your Magic Cap communicator. Maybe you've even got some ideas of your own about what you'd like to see. Until those accessories are available, you can use construction tools yourself to spruce up and personalize your communicator. You've probably guessed by now that there's no end to the messing around you can do customizing your communicator with construction mode and tinkering.

☞ **There's More to Life Than This.** For serious package developers, General Magic offers a powerful computer-based development kit. This kit uses object-oriented programming tools along with Magic Cap's construction features to help programmers build software packages.

Summary

You turn construction mode on with a check box in the general control panel, or temporarily by option-tapping the stamp window's title bar. When you're in construction mode, the stamper image turns into a magic hat and contains not only stamps, but also many other pages of goodies that you can choose from to customize Magic Cap. Construction mode affects what you see in every scene: It adds more tools to the tool holder, more commands to the lamp, and more controls to the control panel. Construction mode lets you use the *move*, *copy*, and *stretch* tools in every scene.

Construction mode gives you components to add to your messages to make them more useful. You can add choice boxes, check boxes, and switches, and you can customize them. You can add custom sounds to any button or other item. You can get special coupons that rearrange the order and features of items on the screen.

Another part of construction is the *tinker* tool, a wrench that's one of the *authoring* tools when you're in construction mode. The wrench lets you look inside items and see their behavior and settings, including their image and sound coupons and check boxes for allowing moving, copying, and stretching.

You can make something movable by tinkering with it, and then use the move tool to put it somewhere else. You can take a stamp's image coupon and use it to customize some other item's image. You can use the construction and tinker tools to change factory settings so that you can make your personal communicator really personal.

Finally

Writing this book was both intriguing and intimidating. The software was so deeply integrated that every time I started an explanation, several other aspects also had to be tied in. Did I mention something in a scenario in Chapter 2 that I didn't explain in depth until Chapter 9? How could I set up practical examples when the software was still changing?

As I used the many features and experimented with different examples so that I could write about them, I found myself getting more and more excited about Magic Cap and how useful it would be in real life. I actually began thinking in terms of having a Magic Cap communicator with me all the time, and how I could use it to schedule meetings, keep addresses handy, jot down notes, and, most important, communicate with people easily and conveniently. Writing this book reaffirmed for me how Magic Cap will change my life, and I tried to share that sense of excitement as I wrote. Magic Cap has great potential to expand and enrich the way people communicate.

Index

Actions
  reversing, 72
  sounds, 4
Addressees
  adding, 43
  multiple, 43
  replacing, 43
  types, 43–44
Addresses, 9
  name cards, 120, 122–123
Addressing commands
  window, 44
Alarm+ button, 104–108
Animation, 3
Anniversaries, 81–82
Announcement window,
  62–63
Appointments
  alarms, 109–110
  customizing, 108–110
  datebook, 80–85
  multi-day, 107
  overlapping, 101–102
  priority, 106–108
  recurring, 83–85
  status, 106–108
Automatic word-
  completion lists,
  228–229

Basics book, 226
Bassett hound and
  searching, 71
Batteries
  displaying status, 222–223
  installing, 3
  viewing level, 68
Birthdays, 80–81
Books
  Basics, 226

creating and editing
  messages, 227
Getting Started, 225–226
marking, 227
power-user features,
  227
putting away, 226
sending messages, 227
table of contents, 226
Bottom of screen lesson,
  14
Business letter
  addressing, 31–32
  customizing, 44–45
  making it standard, 46
  salutation, 30
  sender's name, 30
  sending, 31, 33
Business trips, 97–98
Buttons, 68–74
  alarm+, 104–108
  contact, 70
  desk, 68–69, 220
  fax, 70
  file, 71
  find, 71
  garbage truck, 73–74
  infrared beam, 70
  lamp, 70–72
  mail, 70
  option key and, 74
  print, 71–72
  revert, 72
  stamper, 69
  toolholder, 72–73
  tote bag, 72

Calculator
  attaching tape to
    message, 218
  figuring tips, 218–219

paper tape, 217–218
scientific, 219
Calendar, 214
Choice boxes, 65
  customizing messages,
    236–238
  status, 106
Clock, 212–214
  daylight savings time,
    214
  setting, 212–214
  time zone, 214
Clock scene, 15, 61
Confirmation
  announcement
    window, 63
Construction mode, 75,
  233–246
  adding lamp
    commands, 235
  categories within, 234
  custom forms, 236–239
  magic hat, 234
  on/off, 222
  previewing, 235
  snapshots, 178–179
  sound and image
    customization, 239–240
  sound drawers, 240
  tinker tool, 242–246
  tools for scenes, 234–235
Control panel
  general panel, 221–222
  power panel, 222–223
  privacy panel, 223
  screen panel, 222
  signature panel, 223
  sound effects, 222
Coupons, 16

personalization, 5–6, 9
required setup, 8–11
setting time and date,
  12–13
set up dialing, 10
touch sensitivity, 3
Graphs, 173–175
faxing, 175
labeling, 174
points, 174–175
printing, 175
Groups
adding members, 134–
  135
name cards, 133–137
sending messages to,
  134–135
stamped, 135–137

Hallway, 219–230
control panel, 220–223
desk, 220
directory, 219
game room, 229–230
library, 224–229
listing Magic Cap's
  creators, 230
painting, 230
step-back hand, 219
Help Books package,
  204

Images, customization,
  239, 240
In box, 50–53
announcing in-coming
  mail, 52–53
filing messages, 194–
  195
reading messages then
  filing, 195–199
sorting in-coming
  mail, 53, 192–193
Information
searching for, 71
writing down, 160–161
Information network
  offers, 13–14
Infrared beaming, 41,
  70
Interface, 59

Keyboard. *See* on–screen
  keyboard

Label maker, 47, 73, 76,
  182, 237, 239
Lamp, 70–72
adding buttons, 72
adding commands, 235
Lessons, 6–18
adding signature, 15–
  16
bottom of screen, 14
date and time, 11–13
finishing, 17–18
getting started, 9–14
keyboard, 15
library, 225–226
making phone calls,
  16–17
quitting, 7
sending messages, 16
signing up for
  PersonaLink
  service, 13
top of screen, 14
Library
books, 224–227
lessons, 225–226
Word Lists, 228–229
Lists, 175–180
deleting items, 176
editing, 176
naming, 175
rearranging, 176
sorting, 175
two-column, 179–180

Magic Cap
consistency, 65, 172
development kit, 247
navigation, x, 60–65
personal
  communication and,
  xiv
Magic hat, 234
drawers, 236
Mail button, 70
Meetings
adding names, 87–88
electronic mail
  responses, 92

integration, 93
inviting people, 89–91
postcards, 89–90
prioritizing, 88
responses from
  attendees, 91–92
scheduling, 85–93
selecting attendees,
  86–88
sending messages, 90–
  91
Memory cards, 206–208
archiving data, 206–
  207
extending main
  memory, 207–208
viewing what is stored
  there, 208
Messages
addressees, 43–44
addressing, 26
arriving, 50–53
book on creating and
  editing, 227
choosing tools, 42–43
clearing, 52
creation, 25–26
customizing, 42–47
delivering, 36–41
faxes, 41
filing, 51–52, 195–200
filing rules, 49, 50
forwarding, 28–29, 54,
  238
groups, 134–135
in box, 50–53
infrared beaming, 41
logging, 49
mailing, 27–28
manually filing, 193–
  195
offers from
  information
  networks, 13–14
out box, 47–50
replying, 28–29
return to sender, 39
sending, 24–28
sending lesson, 16
signing, 27
sorting, 51, 196–200